Volunteer Ministries

New Strategies

for

Today's Church

Newton-Cline Press
421 N. Sam Rayburn Fwy.
Sherman, TX 75090
(214) 892-1818

Margie Morris

Newton-Cline Press
421 N. Sam Rayburn Fwy.
Sherman, TX 75090
(214) 892-1818

ISBN 0-9620898-1-8
Volunteer Ministries
New Strategies for Today's Church

If the church does not anchor itself in the will to volunteer, its witness in the world is null and void.

Bishop Bruce P. Blake

Dedicated to my husband, Tim, and my children, Kim, Clay and Grant, who have been known to ask, "And just what is it that you do at that typewriter?"

About the Author

Margie Morris is a nationally known trainer and author. Her newsletter, *Volunteer Impact: New Ideas for Growing Churches*, is read by church leaders all across the country.

A former church staff member, Margie admits to making her share of mistakes in volunteer management. "One of the reasons I can stand up in front of people at our seminars and speak frankly about the subject is that I've experienced it from both sides of the fence."

Margie has a rich history of volunteer service. She currently works as a board member for the Wesley Village Retirement Community, as a public relations committee member for the Grayson County United Way, as a PTA representative in the public schools and as a Sunday School teacher at her church.

Table of Contents

Chapter One

Today's Reality:
What Ever Happened
to June Cleaver?

When love and skill work together,
expect a masterpiece.
John Ruskin

Jesus said, "Feed my sheep."
John 21:17 (KJV)

Even youngsters like me lapse into reminiscences about "the good old days." You know, when baseball bats went "crack" instead of "ping" and gasoline prices enabled us to cruise Highway 82 out by the Dairy Queen. Oreos weren't yet double-stuffed and housewives weren't extinct.

Those of us who grew up in the church recall Sunday evening fellowship suppers with real food that was prepared at home and presented for consumption in wicker baskets with checked napkins. Vacation Bible School was a virtual hotbed of activity involving all the neighborhood children and most of their mothers. Worship was an occasion for hats, gloves, ties, and tight shoes. The church was a natural and pervasive part of our lives.

Now, as adult church leaders, we wonder how everything got so complicated! What happened to commitment? Why is it so difficult to recruit volunteers? When did "church work" cease to be a priority?

Although any learned scientist will testify that the world really isn't hurtling through space any faster than it ever was, we find ourselves contemplating enormous changes at rapid-fire intervals. Sure, every day still has 24 hours in it, but we are subjected to overchoice and bombarded with instant information. "Hurry up" has replaced "Good morning" as the family's most often-heard greeting.

So, while we agree that the last 25 (or even 10) years have brought significant societal changes, you and I both know that--in many cases--the church has not kept up. Especially regarding lay leadership. We've lost people. And we don't know what to do about it.

Volunteer ministries are the heart of the church. It is through involvement and service that we discover and share the best we have to give. It's what brings our theology to life. It's how we recognize the Christ in others and ourselves.

The roots of volunteer service are deeply embedded in our Christian Heritage. In 1 Peter 4:10 (TLB) we read, "God has given each of you some special abilities; be sure to use them to help each other, passing on to others God's many kinds of blessings."

In serving, we respond to God according to our values, beliefs, knowledge and compassion. In the words of Dean Stanley, "The true calling of a Christian is not to do extraordinary things, but to do ordinary things in an extraordinary way."

Jesus walked among the people--teaching, reaching out and comforting. He didn't confine himself to religious issues. He dealt with real problems in a revolutionary way. The risks he took were enormous, ultimately destroying the man. But not the mission.

How did such important work ever get reduced to "Who do you think will do it?" That's "slot filling." As a wide-spread practice, it is destroying potential disciples. Where is the dignity in accepting or serving in a position "because no one else would do it"? The result of such desperation is frustration, burnout or eternal martyrdom.

We can do better than that.

Whether your goal is to develop an exciting new volunteer management plan or revitalize an existing one, this book can help. It is born out of years of research, a multitude of interviews and nitty-gritty experience.

My purpose is to explore issues and exchange information in the hope that what has worked for others might work for you. Supplement these pages with your unique creativity and your own brand of caring. Together, perhaps we can design the key that will open new doors for a new time.

What Are the Possibilities?

Imagine a church with a waiting list of people wanting to teach Sunday School. Or a congregation that prints a booklet for church members listing 145 different volunteer opportunities. Suppose I mentioned a small-town church that provides a legal clinic for those who cannot afford such services.

For those of us who have experienced difficulty "just covering the bases," these shining examples seem nothing short of miraculous. They represent volunteerism in the church at its best. Many of us have seen it at its *worst*. There's a big difference.

How do they do it? If there's a magical abraca-dabra formula, I couldn't find it. Churches with dynamic volunteer programs rely on:

~ a sense of professionalism
~ well-defined goals
~ a sound plan
~ an openness to innovation
~ clergy and staff support
~ a tendency to celebrate success

Revitalization doesn't happen overnight. It's a continuing process of strengthening what is working well and letting go of what isn't. In the church, where tradition is cherished, there must also be a willingness to try new things.

Otherwise, we find ourselves attempting to staff weekday morning Vacation Bible Schools when moms are at work and the kids are in day care. We insist on meeting once a month to discuss building issues when there are no building issues. We plan fellowship meals that nobody wants to cook. We cling to our Sunday morning assembly rituals while every adult under sixty drinks coffee in the hallway.

Why? Because *we've always done it that way*.

That's not meant as a harsh indictment. We all like comfortable houseshoes! But when we perpetuate outdated or ineffective practices because we haven't paused for evaluation or reassessment in 20 years, we find ourselves maintaining the status quo without much imagination or enthusiasm.

Without creative change, where would McDonald's be? Still making nothing but hamburgers under the golden arches instead of serving quick breakfasts to executives-on-the-go. Hospitals would remain dreaded facilities for the sick without stress reduction seminars, exercise classes and wellness clinics. And your local library card would not speak computerese.

It's a different world! Much has changed, including the typical volunteer. There aren't many June Cleavers around any more. It's time we stopped looking for them.

Who is Today's Volunteer?

Take a look around you if you want to discover Today's Volunteer. Notice the corporate executives heading up the United Way campaign. Read the *Newsweek* articles about the disabled coal miner who volunteers sixty hours a week in a West Virginia food pantry. Recall the news story of the twelve-year-old boy who collected blankets to deliver to the homeless.

Volunteers today are male or female, young or old. They come from every economic and cultural background. And they volunteer for *reasons of their own.*

According to a 1988 Independent Sector survey conducted by the Gallup organization, 56% volunteered because they wanted to do something useful. Another 34% enjoyed the nature of the work; 27% wanted to benefit a friend or family member. Only 22% volunteered for what was termed "religious reasons."

What do these new volunteers want?

Many of them bring strong professional and technical skills to their volunteer assignments. They expect to use them. Some hope to add to their job proficiencies or learn something entirely new. To do that, they want appropriate kinds of training and support.

And even though volunteers take their work seriously, they expect at least some aspects of the work to be fun!

By necessity, today's volunteers are more discriminating. They are project-oriented and much more likely to accept short-term assignments than open-ended ones. They enjoy working together as a family. They respond to intergenerational opportunities.

Volunteers want to see themselves as part of an effective team, using their skills to make a difference. Most want to have input into the projects they work on--if not in the planning stages, then later during evaluation. Many expect to participate in goal setting and problem solving.

They want clear, concise information about the jobs they are asked to do.

If we are to attract this new breed of volunteer, those of us who manage and coordinate them must be professional, caring, ethical and efficient. We cannot afford to waste a volunteer's time or abilities.

Sloppy job placement, insufficient support systems and failure to share authority will lose us needed volunteers.

What Difference Does Age Make?

Just as our lifestyles have changed in the past few years, so have age-level demographics. The statistics are startling in their revelations, and they directly affect our programs, projects and people. Volunteer managers face not one or two, but four distinct age groups whose needs and goals they must be aware of and whose special abilities they must learn to deploy.

First of all, we can stop worrying about why the youth group isn't as big as it was in 1965. They're not there because they were never born! For the first time in history, there are more people over the age of 65 than there are teenagers.

And you can forget the addled grandpa on the porch rocker. More likely, grandad took early retirement and has started on a second profession. Or he's sailing the Pacific. Or he's volunteering.

Senior adults today are healthier, more active, and living longer than ever before. They are less dependent on extended family and more likely to be separated geographically from their children and grand-children.

Seniors today are taking college classes and they're teaching them, as well. They have much to offer the church and the community. Although they do seem better able to cook than the rest of us, *perhaps we should call on their talents for other things besides food preparation!*

After the over 65 generation, comes what national trainer and consultant, Marlene Wilson, de-scribes as "the sandwich generation"--that group who have raised their own children into young adulthood and are now "parenting" older parents. Sometimes, they're still parenting their grown children, as well. The much ballyhooed "empty nest" may give way to a *return* to the nest by offspring unable to make it on their own.

Many women of the sandwich generation volunteered innumerable hours during their homemak-ing years. They can organize, execute and clean up with a flourish. Some of these post-World War II moms have pursued postponed careers, gone back to school or turned their volunteer experience into gainful employ-ment. They, along with their husbands who probably once served as Scout masters and Little League coaches, can bring experience and expertise to volunteer programs.

Adults of this age are often pillars of the church. They have spent a lifetime caring for others, and they deserve more than gold stars for their service.

The third group, the "Baby Boomers," are still around in force, but until recently, have been largely absent from our churches. Born between 1946 and 1964, this group comprises one third of the U.S. population. Not known for their willingness to play by the rules, many Boomers profess no denominational loyalty.

These young adults look for quality packaging. They expect relevance, meaningful interactions, efficiency, a little glitz and a sense of humor.

The nationwide shift toward regular church attendance that we are beginning to see now comes at a time when Boomers are reassessing their values, seeking Christian education for their children and a renewed spiritual awareness for themselves. In an article in *Discipleship Trends*, Warren J. Hartman says, "An encouraging note is that the fastest growth areas among most major denominations is due to the return of the baby boomers who are also bringing their children. They are giving us a second chance. It is very unlikely that we will have a third one."

Finally, we cannot afford to overlook the fourth group--teenagers and children--as potential volunteers. Their capabilities far exceed emptying trash baskets or painting Easter eggs. We label them "unreliable" because we entrust them with low-responsibility, boring jobs and they get discouraged and quit. You and I would too.

Volunteer service gives young people a chance to succeed at an age when self-esteem is often rocky. Their real contributions bring recognition and appreciation. By inviting them to volunteer, we convey confidence and trust. They seldom disappoint us.

As we incorporate children and teenagers as full partners in our volunteer efforts, we must never ask them to do anything we would not ask of an adult. If the job is "childish," expand it, redesign it or throw it out!

Who Needs What?

Of course the church has positions to fill and programs to run. But when we operate from the church-as-organization-that-must-have-volunteers-to-function perspective, we lose sight of the volunteer's needs. Then we lose volunteers.

Who are the people in your congregation? Why do they volunteer? Or why don't they? What are their interests? What do they do well? What would they like to learn?

Consider your church. How effective is your volunteer program? What kinds of support are given on a continuing basis? How diverse are the jobs available? What opportunities does the church provide for work in the community?

We can't sit back, operate lackadaisical programs and assume that church members will volunteer because they're *supposed* to. They won't.

It's important to be realistic about what motivates volunteers. Otherwise, we might put Mary in charge of keeping the church supply room well stocked and organized when what she really wanted from volunteering was to meet new friends. Mary would be disappointed, as would Tom, the self-proclaimed neatnik who thrives on bringing order out of chaos, but whom we overlooked when we gave the job to Mary.

When a group of church members was asked to give some of the reasons why they chose to volunteer, their responses were, in no particular order:

1. the opportunity to be creative
2. the chance to advocate certain causes
3. a need to be heard
4. the desire to become more competent
5. a feeling of responsibility (or guilt)
6. a need for information--to know what's going on
7. exposure to new people, new ideas
8. the prospect of having influence
9. an inability to say "no"
10. a wish to give something back--

to the church or community
11. the need to belong
12. a special affinity for the work.

And, although nobody is going to report a need for high visibility or a desire for power as a reason for volunteering, these motivations, too, are legitimate and common.

You can interview potential volunteers about their needs and expectations as a step in the process of effective placement. Learn what each individual's needs are and respond to them. It's better than guessing.

Your "power person" could be a great project chair, able to organize and delegate to get the job done. Your "high visibility person" would probably welcome the chance to serve as public relations liaison between the church and community agencies. There is a person for every job and a job for every person.

Why Facilitate Community Involvement?

Community agencies? We have enough trouble getting people to help in the church. Why should we offer them the chance to work somewhere else?

Because we are commissioned to become the scattered church. Because ministry is not confined to within church walls. Because a healthy church is an advocate in the world, not an audience.

Churches with strong volunteer outreach programs are generally healthy, growing and vibrant. They attract new members who want to be part of the action. Their volunteer job opportunities are numerous and varied. Their mission statement is more than a string of words--it's a way of living.

Active service brings renewed vitality. Projects that encompass global concerns, community issues, health care, racial justice, crisis intervention, child abuse prevention, the environment and world peace allow the work of the church to be the work of the world.

Call your Volunteer Action Center or local non-profit agencies to find out how you can link your volunteer program with their services. It benefits everybody.

What Does an Effective Program Look Like?

The best volunteer management systems don't just happen. Neither do they simply fall into place with one initial push. They evolve as a result of considerable effort, careful planning and constant nurturing.

Listen in on the thought processes that produce a successful program. Listen to the congregation of West Side Presbyterian Church in Ridgewood, New Jersey:

> *Several years ago we made a decision as a congregation to seek together a deeper relationship with Jesus Christ. As the first century church did it, so did we; by committing ourselves to do one activity in the areas of Renewal, Reaching Out and Rejoicing. Those of us who have pursued this discipline are discovering that we are finding a new joy and strength for living.*

The people of this congregation combined their deeply-felt theological beliefs with practical day-to-day applications that enabled every member to be in ministry. Here's how they describe the volunteer program that emerged:

> *The purpose of the volunteer ministries program is to actualize our theology of the priesthood of all believers. We at West Side affirm that every member is a minister, endowed with special gifts. We believe that as we share these gifts and minis-*

tries, our common life is enriched and our mission in the community enhanced. The goal is threefold...

> ** to enable each person in the congregation to discover his or her own gifts and to share them with others in the church and/or community;*
> ** to improve and coordinate our systems of recruiting, training and supporting volunteers;*
> ** to match the needs of Boards, Councils and committees with identified gifts and interests.*

It is not another program to compete with existing ministries, but rather, through the staff coordinator and the committee, it is the one program intended to enable all the others. (From *Renew, Rejoice, Reach Out*, a booklet published for volunteers at West Side Presbyterian Church, Ridgewood, New Jersey.)

We have work to do! In renewing our volunteer programs, we revitalize the entire church. We must uplift volunteer ministries within and beyond the church so that opportunities for service are purposeful, clearly defined and well organized. The time has come for us to roll up our sleeves, put on our aprons and feed His sheep.

Chapter Two

Just Do It:
An Action Plan

*We must be clear about our reasons for
both being and doing, or church work becomes just another activity to squeeze in (if
we must) or get out of (if we can).*
Marlene Wilson

When there is no vision, the people perish....
Proverbs 29:18 (KJV)

Once the decision is made to develop and acti-
vate a strong volunteer ministries program, our tendency
is to:

a) jump out and recruit as many people as we
    can to fill as many jobs as we can, or
b) begin to call meetings, assemble design teams
    and contemplate objectives.

When we start without a plan, things go haywire.
Then we whine, "Well, we tried, but it just didn't work!"
Or the opposite may occur. We may get so bogged

down in the plan that nothing much ever happens. After a while, we forget what we were called to do in the first place.

You know your congregation. Chances are, you can develop a master plan tailored to your church. But if you need some footholds to get you started, this chapter should spark a few ideas.

Work within the framework of your church. Don't be intimidated by it. Find out what your boundaries are. If you need to get approval from your church's governing body, be forthright and clear about what you are asking for. Invite and listen to differing opinions. Whether you are clergy, staff, or a member of the laity, you will want to work with others to share information, gather resources and develop a realistic program that will work for *your* church.

Why a Team Effort?

The process of elevating volunteer ministries to a top priority involves a tremendous commitment. If it was as easy as simply "deciding to do better," we'd all have top-notch programs. No matter how capable you are, you'll need help.

Ask the Parish Council, the Nominating Committee, the Administrative Board, or whatever decision-making body functions in your church to solicit volunteers to serve on a task force. This group may need to meet regularly for as long as a year before evolving into a Volunteer Ministries Committee, or some such team that will nourish and sustain the foundation you lay.

Determine how the task force will fit into the structure of your church and what measures of accountability will be observed. Remember that the volunteer ministries program is one that enables all other committees, commissions and projects to remain fully staffed and productive.

Since you're the one reading this book, nominate yourself to chair the task force! You will want to make periodic reports to whatever assembly has sanctioned the team. The group will be more effective (and happier) if it is composed of "at-large" members and is not just a compilation of other chairpeople. You'll want a good mix of personalities and perspectives. And don't forget to include a variety of age levels. It will be more fun that way!

Make it a priority to keep the congregation informed about the activities of the task force. The unknown can make people apprehensive, and we all tend to be a little nervous when we sense something significant is about to happen. If we're invited to participate in the process, or at least given information about it, we become less anxious than if we're left to our own imaginings. Planning *with* people is always preferable to planning *for* them.

What About a Mission Statement?

What do we believe about why we are here? Every decision you make about volunteer ministries--every project you start, every job description you write--is an outgrowth of your mission. The mission affects how you deal with problems, how you communicate with people, how you structure your programs and how you interact with volunteers. It clarifies your purpose and directs your actions.

Your task force will want to write a mission statement for your volunteer ministries program. You may want to adapt your church's general mission statement. Or you may decide to come up with something

The Volunteer Ministries Task Force

ADMINISTRATIVE BOARD

COUNCIL ON MINISTRIES

VOLUNTEER MINISTRIES PROGRAM

COMMITTEES COMMISSIONS WORK PROJECTS

Here's how your volunteer ministries program might fit into your church's governing structure.

entirely different. Invite other staff members, as well as volunteer leaders and task force members to deliberate with you.

Address this question: *Why volunteer in our church?*

Writer's block? Explain how volunteering is connected to your theology. Discuss the use of spiritual gifts. Link volunteer ministries with the total church mission. Then, using simple, straightforward language, develop a statement that is both inspirational and practical. Try to say exactly what you mean in no more than 50 words.

Here's what it might look like:

> *At Glenbrook Church, volunteer programs broaden our ministry by offering opportunities for service in the church and community. We encourage all persons to use their God-given gifts and unique talents that we might become the scattered church, responding to God's love as modern disciples in today's world.*

Once the group has shared opinions and insights, made revisions and received approvals, PROCLAIM YOUR MESSAGE!

Print copies for distribution as worship bulletin inserts.

Highlight the words in the church newsletter.

Tack a flyer on the bulletin board.

Make certificates bearing the mission statement and give one to every volunteer.

A mission statement helps us focus on why we are "in business" in the first place. It's a powerful motivator and a useful guide.

How Can We Broaden Our Vision?

There are unmet needs both inside and outside the church. Allow your task force the luxury of brainstorming in an upbeat, crazy, anything is possible atmosphere. Have your meetings at a coffee shop, under a tree or in someone's den. Supply pencils with funny erasers, use colored notepads and eat ice cream. From this innovative approach (which might change the way we conduct church meetings forever!) will come new ideas and sound suggestions for exciting ministries within the church and the community.

Think about what it is you are asking your volunteers to do. As long as you don't wear silly hats, there's nothing unprofessional about informal meetings. One major U.S. corporation provides a specially-designed room to allow top employees to get away from the buzz of office machines and do some creative thinking. Your church probably doesn't have such a room, so you'll have to improvise!

It makes good sense to enlarge the scope of volunteer opportunities to include many different kinds of work that can be performed in a variety of settings at flexible times. We also want to "build into the system" ways to utilize exceptional talents offered by individuals. Give some thought to how the church might use Uncle Fred's prize-winning hog calls or little Clarissa's bent for the trombone in your church activities.

Imagine the response if you requested help in a wide variety of areas. What could you add to the list on the next page:

Special Volunteer Skills

gardening
kitchen crew
bulletin board
 designer
choir booster
photographer
nurse
clown ministry
musical
instrument-
 alist
aerobics
cake decorating
painting
sewing and needle-
 work
wedding coordinator
publicity
floral arranging
office assistants
interviewing

storytelling
camping
worship assistants
vehicle maintenance
nature specialists
single adult fellow-
 ship
parent education
nursing home
 visitors
retreat planners
recovery support
 team
costume designer
computer
 programmer
choir member
Communion assist-
 ants
food bank workers

You can see how people might initially become involved in such activities to pursue a hobby, learn a new skill, meet with friends or get some exercise. Volunteer service is a natural outgrowth of these kinds of activities. Sewing costumes for the Christmas play, designing a flyer for the church chili supper or providing a blood pressure check are just a few ways that interests, hobbies and professional abilities can be used in volunteer work. Besides including more people, these broader volunteer roles add sparkle and a little pizzazz to every area of church life.

Your task force will also want to discuss extending volunteer opportunities outside the church. You may choose to develop your own community projects. Or you may want to link services with other local agencies. Coordinate carefully to prevent duplicated efforts.

The number of agencies needing volunteers is growing every day. Be alert for requests for help in the newspaper, on television and radio. See how your church can support community projects. On the next page, you'll find a list of possibilities to get you started.

Community Projects

Boy Scouts
Big Sisters
prison inmates
crisis centers
drug prevention
Meals on Wheels
tutoring
home hospice
Special Olympics
soup kitchens
Red Cross
wildlife pre-
  servation
homeless shelters
bilingual preschools
home repairs for
  the elderly
substance abuse
legal assistance
senior day care
youth centers
support groups
hospital aux-
  iliaries
refugee reset-
  tlement

Aren't Volunteers Free?

Because volunteers donate their time, we sometimes assume that the programs and projects they staff are cost-free.

Surprise!

They're not. Your task force will want to determine a proposed budget to include a variety of expenses not presently covered by allocated funds.

You might consider funding child care for your workers, training expenses, necessary resources, reimbursement for the volunteer's out-of-pocket costs and money for recognition and appreciation. Record-keeping requires the use of office equipment and supplies. Your church may want to produce a newsletter, which would incur copying and postage expenses.

Ask the task force to review the church's insurance policy, to see that there is adequate coverage for volunteer workers.

This is a good time to introduce the question of program coordination. Even in a small-membership church, a "Coordinator of Volunteer Ministries" is essential. In larger congregations with multiple staff members, a "Director of Volunteer Ministries" may be required.

If the position will be a staff responsibility in your church, will it be full or part time? What recommendations will the task force make about salary? In Chapter Three, we will take a more comprehensive look at the volunteer coordinator position and examine what options might work best for your church.

If your eyebrows are coming together under the weight of this financial conversation, consider this. A recent national survey conducted by Gallup for Independent Sector showed that 36% of those in religious organizations felt that *they were not giving enough!* Another major finding of this report suggests that giving could be increased if volunteering were increased. A dynamic volunteer ministries program is something you can't afford *not* to have.

How Will You Gather Information?

How will you know what Susan is good at? Does Fred still grow a bountiful vegetable garden each spring? Would Marie consider coordinating a day camp for fifth and sixth graders? Is John comfortable playing his guitar in front of a group of people? How many projects is Jean currently involved with? Did the Thompson family take slides during their visit to the Holy Land?

The best way to find out about people and what they are willing to share with the church is to ask them. How you will do that is something the task force might discuss.

Some churches use "time and talent" surveys. Others send interviewing teams out to visit each family in the congregation. Some take telephone surveys. Some tie in their volunteer identification efforts with the annual stewardship campaign. Some solicit information in "new member packets" or through the mail.

Use whatever procedure will work well for your church. Just be sure that once the information is gathered, it is put to use!

Acknowledge receipt of responses immediately. We do a terrible disservice when we ask about an individual's gifts or areas of interest and then never follow up on the information. Whether you enter the data into a computer or file it on index cards, reply quickly to all who respond. Say thank you!

Your task force can decide how best to use the information given and how to ensure that the material is continually updated. It's a big job and you'll want to leave it in capable hands.

How Do We Get Moving?

There are several schools of thought regarding the charting of action plans. One includes developing intricate strategies and subtle techniques. One involves goals and objectives, another, design models or checks and balances.

Why not throw caution to the wind and just decide where you want to go and how you hope to get there? You want to be realistic, of course, and decide on manageable steps that will move your church logically and progressively toward your vision. But that shouldn't be terribly difficult!

We in the church are often overly cautious-- afraid of failure, disapproval or lack of permission. I'm not advocating running roughshod over people and existing programs. Rather, I'm a believer in action. I think we can over-talk, over-legislate and ultimately defeat valid advancements. If we wait for all the stars to be in alignment, we'll spend a long time waiting.

You can help create a climate for success. Share your vision. Utilize the committees and commissions already in place within your church. Ask for input. Solicit help. Delegate. Hold workers accountable. Publicize every step. Celebrate all accomplishments. Invite involvement at every opportunity.

Your efforts merit quality attention. The revitalization deserves the support and prayers of the congregation. Peter Drucker says that good leaders "look up from their work and outward toward goals." The vision you and your task force inspire will motivate your congregation toward the rich rewards of service and the personal satisfaction of discipleship.

The Volunteerism Committee Statement on the following page is reproduced with the permission of the Volunteerism Committee, Our Saviour's Lutheran Church, Merrill, Wisconsin.

VOLUNTEERISM COMMITTEE

The purpose of the volunteerism committee is to create a more effective ministry of volunteers. A Volunteer Coordinator and Assistant Volunteer Coordinator--who serve for two-year terms--coordinate and continuously bring together volunteers from committees that have needs for service.

The volunteerism committee which became operational in 1982 has taken several training sessions and divided into subcommittees to implement and share volunteerism techniques. The various duties of the committee are:

(1) to prepare volunteer ministry position descriptions so every committee member has a clear expectation of what it is they are to accomplish;

(2) to identify volunteers in the congregation and keep a central record available for committee use;

(3) to match volunteers and ministry positions, maximizing the use of all who wish to volunteer and integrating them into the mainstream of church life;

(4) to orient and train volunteers;

(5) to recognize volunteer service work in the congregation and in the community;

(6) to help volunteers experience growth by moving from one commitment to another through evaluation;

(7) to be alert to Volunteerism needs and opportunities in the congregation and bring these to the attention of the Church Council and Committees.

The Volunteer Coordinator forms an easily identified contact for anyone that has volunteer needs in their area. Whatever interest anyone may have in looking through the various opportunities in church volunteer ministry listed in this publication, the Volunteer Coordinator can put you in touch with the right person. The church newsletter regularly lists the Volunteer Coordinators' phone numbers, or call the church office.

Chapter Three

Management: What's a Volunteer Coordinator to Do?

When the best leader's work is done, the people say, "We did it ourselves."
                                Lao-Tzu

It was he (Christ) who gave some to be apostles, some to be prophets, some to be evangelists, and some to be pastors and teachers, to prepare God's people for works of service...
                                Ephesians 4:11-12 (NIV)

    Autopilot may guide a 747, but it's a lousy way to run a volunteer program. Few would consider having a choir without a director, but somehow we expect volunteer ministries to function by themselves. The truth is that, even if you do succeed in launching a model project, you will have difficulty sustaining it without professional leadership. You need a volunteer coordinator.

Don't make the mistake of assuming that the pastor, church secretary or the chair of the Volunteer Committee can do the job. No matter how capable any of these folks may be, they have other important responsibilities. A successful volunteer ministries program requires sound management and attention to detail. The person in charge must have specific abilities and the necessary skills to keep the program healthy. It's a tall order.

Once a church makes the commitment to strengthen and expand volunteer opportunities, many do decide to invest in a full or part time director. Your task force can decide what is best for your congregation and then make a recommendation to the church's governing body.

Choose a title that reflects the key managerial role the position requires. Some churches have a "director of ministries," a "congregational care coordinator" or a "volunteer coordinator." Design the job as a professional position. Grant the authority and accessibility necessary for effective leadership.

"Our volunteer coordinator serves as an outspoken advocate to the Council on Ministries and the Administrative Board," one church leader explained. "She keeps us aware of changing needs, program goals and the volunteer's perspectives. She sees that we stay informed about on-going projects. And she keeps the volunteer programs in tune with the whole church."

Experienced volunteer directors say that a coordinator offers an important connection among the congregation, the clergy and the lay leaders.

A director of a thriving Milwaukee program says, "My position keeps people from falling through the cracks or sliding out the backdoor." She defines her role as "meeting the challenge of helping people find volunteer jobs, helping them feel a part of the Body of Christ."

What, Exactly, Does the Director Do?

Mike Murray, a Presbyterian pastor and church consultant, equates the position to that of personnel director in any corporation or business. The director's job is to make the best use of the resources available. In the church, that responsibility also includes helping volunteers experience the Gospel. A good manager helps volunteers see themselves as worthwhile, significant and loved. Finally, Murray says volunteer managers can motivate the church to reclaim the work of its people, both within and outside the walls of the church.

Your task force will develop an initial job description for the director. It will change and grow as your program does. Here are some basic job-functions to help you get started in writing the job description for your director:

(1) Coordinate volunteer projects with all church programs and projects.

(2) Maintain accurate records.

(3) Write and update job descriptions.

(4) Discover and make use of individual gifts.

(5) Coordinate work projects and committee functions.

(6) Interview/Place/Train volunteers.

(7) Manage the program budget.

(8) Design recruitment and recognition approaches.

(9) Market volunteer opportunities.

(10) Link church and community events.

If this sounds like a 60-hour-a-week job, remind yourself (and perhaps your director occasionally) that he or she will not necessarily be *doing* the work, but rather seeing that it gets done. How that is accomplished depends on your church and your director.

Volunteers are an essential part of operating your volunteer management program. Use their talents however you can. It will strengthen the church and save the director's sanity.

For example, in one church a retired personnel director conducts interviews. A high school student comes in after school to enter data into the computer. An ad copywriter assists with publicity. They have become a management team that practices what it preaches!

If we depend on one person to do all and be all things, we set ourselves and others up for disappointment. Even the most multi-talented can do only so many things well at a time. If we force our director into being "a doer" to the point of excess, that person can become a bottleneck rather than a bridge to expansion and diversity.

How Do You Write a Job Description?

Initially, your task force will want to provide job descriptions for key positions. Later the volunteer director and members of the Volunteer Committee will work together to design and update a more complete file.

In many cases, churches either don't have any job

descriptions for volunteers, or use the prepared versions distributed from faraway conference offices. Both approaches are equally ineffective.

By failing to provide job descriptions, we assume that everyone knows what to do (which also implies that the job will be done the same way year after year). Or we excuse ourselves by saying that without rigid guidelines, volunteers can do whatever they want.

When we use "canned" versions, we rubber-stamp jobs. The models we use may have little to do with our local church. Pre-written job descriptions are helpful when used as guidelines, but frustrating when taken as law.

A job description doesn't tell a volunteer *how* to do a job. It simply defines the position. It gives the information necessary for someone to function successfully in a specific role. One hopes that it also relates the responsibility to the overall mission of the church.

Below are two examples of job descriptions that work. Ask to see the ones that community agencies in your area use. Or call your denomination's regional office for assistance.

Sample Job Description (1)

JOB TITLE: Bulletin Board Designer

RESPONSIBLE TO: Volunteer Director

JOB DESCRIPTION: To be responsible for changing each of the three bulletin boards in the North Wing at least once per quarter.

(1) Bulletin board themes should reflect a current subject of study, a seasonal design, age-level events, teacher appreciation, etc.

(2) Work should be accomplished at some time other than Sunday morning.

        (3) Supplies are to be stored in the
            Resource Room.

        (4) Purchases over $20 must be cleared
            with the Volunteer Director.

TIME REQUIRED: Approximately 6-8 hours per
            quarter.

RESOURCES PROVIDED: Bulletin Board design
            books, art supplies, stapler, scissors, etc.

SKILLS NEEDED: Ability to use imagination and
            creativity in design and theme. Work
            within assigned budget.

TERM: One year

                    * * * * *

Sample Job Description (2)

JOB TITLE: Elementary Sunday School Teacher

RESPONSIBLE TO: Elementary Coordinator

JOB DESCRIPTION: To further the church's mission
        of sharing the love and message of Jesus Christ
        with children of elementary-school age through
        study, fellowship, games and related activities,
        worship and prayer.

        (1) Plan and lead a class of students each Sunday,
            using the United Methodist curriculum
            materials as the primary teaching re-
            source.
        (2) Keep accurate attendance records.
        (3) Turn in names of those absent more than
            three consecutive times to the Education
            Coordinator for appropriate followup.
        (4) Arrange for a substitute from the attached
            substitute-teaching list in the event that
            you cannot be present.
        (5) Inform the Elementary Coordinator if you
            plan a special activity that we might help
            publicize.
        (6) Keep your classroom in good order and sup-

plies well stocked.
(7) Spend time each week in prayer for your
      students and their families.

TIME REQUIRED: Approximately 2 and 1/2 hours
      per week

TRAINING OPPORTUNITIES:
      Conference Teacher
            Workshops
      Skill Building videos
      Reference Library
      Guest Speakers

SKILLS NEEDED:
      Commitment to children, ability to
      share faith experiences, willingness to
      learn, capacity to have fun.

TERM: One quarter

Volunteers need permission to do what they would *like* to do as well as what they are expected to do. Make plans to see that each volunteer receives a personal visit along with the job description. Encourage innovation. Invite input. Set the stage for success.

When you offer a job description as a general guideline, you specify a purpose and a direction without insisting on a particular route. For example, the chairperson for Family Ministries might be asked to plan and implement the following:

1. three intergenerational fellowship
    activities

2. a special Mother's Day and Father's
    Day celebration

3. two seminars of interest to parents

4. one holiday event

The chairperson is not restricted to providing only these activities. Nor is he or she strictly bound by these guidelines. A creative chairperson might be brimming with ideas for family gatherings and decide to initiate a game night. Perhaps a special community event would warrant group discount tickets for church members. Maybe the Family Ministries Committee would rather provide one spectacular parent seminar, rather than two.

Note! There will be times when a job description will reflect an unusual or specific talent. Be prepared to make use of individual gifts. Find ways to allow people to serve by doing what they want to do. Assist a desk-bound executive who would like to coach an inner-city children's basketball team. Allow a graduate student to conduct an internship at the church, serving transients and the homeless. Open the door to all avenues of volunteer service, and be ready for unexpected blessings!

Why Conduct Interviews?

Although interviews are common in the business world, we are often suspicious of them in the church. After all, volunteers are not employees. Why subject church members to an inquisition?

First of all, an interview is simply an effective way to exchange information. It provides a vital link in the placement process. A conversation that helps the volunteer director learn what it is that the volunteer would like to do goes a long way toward effective recruitment and job design.

Perhaps it is the word itself rather than the actual process that makes us uneasy. We are nervous about the prospect of being interrogated, Mike Wallace style. Or we recall the nausea that made our last job interview less than pleasant. So, let's use the word "interview" in a context of caring and genuine interest.

Ivan H. Scheier, Ph.D., Director of the Center for Creative Community in Santa Fe New Mexico says, "We can unravel relevant motivation for volunteering without deep-probing or subtly psyching people. We need just ask them in a caring way, then trust them to tell us what we need to know about their work-relevant motivations."

Consider the interview a chance for the volunteer director or other representative from the volunteer program to establish a rapport with potential volunteers. It's as much a time to answer questions as it is to ask them. Once we dispense with the image of blinding spotlights and bamboo shoots under the fingernails, we can get about the business of getting to know and appreciate volunteers.

Conduct interviews in person, by phone, or even through the mail. Invite potential volunteers to lunch, go by their office or meet them at a ball game. Find a good balance between being volunteer need to keep in mind.

Decide what it is you need to know to match the volunteer with a job that he or she will enjoy. Non-threatening, open-ended questions work best:

> "What were some of the things you liked about your former volunteer jobs?"
>
> "What skills would you like most to use in your volunteer work?"
>
> "Are you comfortable in leadership roles or do you prefer serving on committees?"
>
> "What do you dislike doing?"
>
> "What work settings appeal to you?"

"How much time would you like to donate?"

"How could we help?"

Listen to what the volunteer is saying. Build on the responses given, rather than rushing through your own agenda. For example, if Tom's last volunteer job was in the local theater, invite him to tell you about his experiences there.

Briefly describe the range of volunteer opportunities your church provides. See what has appeal and what doesn't. Investigate the possibility of creating a new position. Give yourself and the volunteer time to think about several alternatives before making a final decision together.

If there is more than a few days time-lapse between the interview and the placement, follow up with a phone call or letter thanking the volunteer for his or her time and interest. Be sure the information you gathered is properly assimilated and recorded for future use.

The interview serves a valuable purpose, but it is only one step in a process of continual interaction with volunteers. Rather than "signing them up and turning them loose," the volunteer director will ensure that volunteers are included in planning, evaluating and building the program. That's why the director must be visible and accessible.

Besides the initial interview, the director may conduct exit interviews, as well. We mustn't be afraid to ask for (and accept) honest feedback. Receive suggestions graciously. Resolve grievances when possible (see Chapter Eight). See that the discussion ends on a positive note.

Keep in mind that sometimes volunteers simply

need to rest.   The words, "How can we serve you?" send a powerful message to the exhausted volunteer. Stay in touch.

What's the Key to Problem-Free Placement?

Susan wonders why she has never been asked to serve on the finance committee. She knows that her ineptness with a checkbook is a secret outside her immediate family. She owns a three-piece suit and wears it to church on occasion. She welcomes challenges and would relish the chance to engage in stimulating conversation.

But because Susan is a homemaker with two small children, she only gets asked to teach the kindergarten Sunday School class, "take her turn" one Sunday a quarter in the nursery, bake cookies for the auction and supervise a booth at the All Saints Day carnival.

She'd like to serve in another capacity totally unrelated to children, but she hesitates to say so, because a) she's not sure she's really qualified, b) she might be perceived as "pushy" or c) "they" might laugh.

This wouldn't happen to Susan at your church. When you have done your homework (i.e. information gathering through survey or interview), you will know what it is Susan might like to start doing and what it is she wants to stop doing. You would know useful things about other people, too.

For instance, your conversation with John revealed that he is proud of his amateur photography awards and would probably jump at the chance to capture the drama of the annual Christmas pageant on film. (You also know that three of his children are scheduled to be angels in the performance.) You won't ask Becky to cook supper for the youth dinner simply because she's the mother of a fifteen-year-old. You are aware that Ted's elderly mother has been ill, requiring a great deal of his time. You wonder if he would appreciate having a substitute bus driver until he recovers some of his own energy.

You can see that placement is so much more than just filling slots. When our programs operate with integrity and an awareness of our volunteers as people, service becomes an exciting option rather than a tiresome duty.

Another aid to effective placement is accurate recordkeeping. You need to know how many projects or positions a volunteer is pursuing at any one time.

What about those who aren't involved? Has anyone contacted new members? Are absentees left to return on their own accord? What committee needs another member?

Hopefully, you have this information available to you on a computer disk. It's faster and easier than a file cabinet with sticky drawers or index cards that are never in order.

Whatever method you use, categorize and cross-reference so that you can locate potential volunteers and support current ones. If you keep volunteer histories up to date, you can readily see that asking Gail to supply helium balloons for Promotion Sunday is probably not a good idea, since she teaches Sunday School and sings in the choir. Frank, on the other hand, is a member of Children's Council and provided party decorations on Valentine's Day. Ask him instead.

Can Volunteers Be Fired?

Most serious problems that arise with volunteers have more to do with "us" than "them." If we coerce people into jobs they don't want, abandon them to sink or swim, and refuse to acknowledge their presence for ten or fifteen years, we can cultivate some angry volunteers. If we fail to visit with prospective volunteers before we place them, we're gambling on the outcome. If *we* do the planning and ask others to carry out *our* wishes, we're likely to foster resentment and resistance.

You can probably list other ways that we sabotage our own programs. In extreme cases, an unhappy volunteer (or a misplaced one) can eventually alienate co-workers and devastate a program. Because we're often not sure what the problem is and are reluctant to "stir things up," we let a situation go on indefinitely, hoping it will get better by itself. It won't.

Once in a great while, despite our best efforts and careful planning, a volunteer is incapable or unwilling to perform his or her duties satisfactorily. Perhaps Joanna agreed to deliver hot lunches to the homebound, but repeatedly failed to show up. Maybe Roy accepted the position of acolyte director, but due to personal problems, did not have the patience or understanding needed to work well with children.

Tackle the problem before it gets to the point where feelings are hurt and folks begin to drop out. If we try to protect one volunteer and lose ten, we haven't gained anything. It's not good for the church, the volunteer program or the people involved. If you handle it before it becomes a major crisis, so much the better.

The volunteer director, pastor or other church leader will want to talk directly *to* the volunteer, not *about* him or her. Address the situation and the behavior that needs changing. Of course, you won't demean the volunteer or the co-workers. Engage the volunteer in problem-solving with you. Listen to what the volunteer has to say. Decide together what steps you both will take to alleviate the problem. Agree to meet again on a specific date to evaluate the situation and see if a satisfactory solution has been reached.

If the necessary changes are not implemented in the time period suggested, you will have to call it as you see it and relieve or, hopefully, reassign the volunteer.

Your approach is critical. You are not a parent assigning punishment, but a manager moving in a decisive direction to restore health to an ailing program and perhaps make better use of the volunteer's gifts. To do so is a caring gesture, accomplished in a quiet, matter-of-fact way.

Affirm the volunteer, who most assuredly had good intentions. Be aware that, despite your best efforts, a troubled volunteer may refuse to serve again, may even leave the church. Nobody likes to see that happen. However, if we refuse to address the problem clearly and directly, we are setting the stage for widespread dissatisfaction. And if we continue to "rescue" the volunteer, we frustrate ourselves and alienate others. It's tough, but sometimes leadership calls for courage.

Can We Coordinate Without a Director?

If a lack of church funds prohibits employing a full time or even part time director, you will want to explore other alternatives.

Small-membership churches might use a "volunteer" volunteer director, or a team of volunteer co-directors. Either way, a Volunteer Committee is essential. Responsibilities will need to be broken down into manageable jobs that each member can perform. Coordination of the coordinators will make the difference between calm and chaos.

Another tactic brings all current committee chairs and group leaders in as department volunteer directors. The head of the Parish Council or church board would decide how best to structure the various functions of a volunteer director's position.

The next suggestion probably requires me to take cover before making it. As a last resort, you could ask members of the current staff to assume a small portion of the management for the program. Some responsibilities can piggyback others; for instance, when the pastor calls on church members, he or she could include an interview about volunteer service.

However, decide what it is you will permit staff members to *stop* doing before you consider asking them to take on these new responsibilities. Most of them work long hours, seldom get rich and often suffer burnout at the hands of demanding congregations. If you decide to ask anyway, don't tell them I gave you the idea!

Obviously, my bias is that all volunteers deserve the caring attention of a capable director. Your program is handicapped without one. Your creative genius may be able to compensate to some extent, but if your goal is an outstanding volunteer ministries program, you will find ways to staff and fund it. Give it your best.

Chapter Four

Involvement:
Make it Easy to Say Yes

*Use what talents you possess; the woods would
be very silent if no birds sang there except
those that sang best.*

Henry Van Dyke

*Now you are the body of Christ, and each
one of you is a part of it.*

I Cor. 12:27 (NIV)

It is our nature to want to be included. We all
recall what it was like as a child when it came time to
choose up sides for a game. As teenagers, we longed to
fit in with the popular crowd. And as adults, we look for
acceptance in our work and our friendships. No one
wants to feel excluded. So why don't our volunteer
programs have waiting lists of people wanting to serve?

Frankly, we put people off. If sloppy management doesn't discourage volunteerism, the stalwart

crowd that "knows how things are done" may do so. It could be that our programs are so fraught with duty, we forget that they can be fun. We sometimes leave potential volunteers out, simply by refusing to climb into their shoes and see ourselves from a different perspective.

It's not just visitors and brand new church members who want to know "How do I fit in here?" We all do! Do you recall asking yourself, "What can I give to this church, this ministry, this community?" Maybe you came up with an idea, but it didn't match the opportunities offered. So you did what the church asked you to do, but the fit never felt right, like shoes two sizes too small.

We spend a lot of energy trying to get people involved. We bemoan the lack of commitment when our efforts don't work. We resort to cajoling, coercing, begging and , occasionally, snarling. Even if we succeed in intimidating volunteers into service, the association is not a happy one. We're like riders spurring our horses onward while tightly holding back on the reins.

Mission motivates. Every recruitment technique imaginable will not bring people in to work for a cause they care nothing about. Our strength lies in fostering the connectedness between faith and action, while allowing volunteers to serve in a ministry of their own choosing.

Our sparkle comes from spotting gifts, developing potential and recognizing God's hand in the work we do. Our sustenance comes from managing our volunteer programs with caring professionalism and from uplifting our efforts in prayer.

How Do We Sabotage Our Own Programs?

Nobody intentionally sets out to sabotage a volunteer effort. Sometimes disappointment is the result of unaware behavior. Occasionally, we do ourselves in by not being clear about what we hope to achieve.

Here's an example. This is a story about Mark and Mary and Jeff and Jenny. Both couples are parents of teenagers. Concerned about dwindling attendance at church youth functions, the four of them decided one day to sponsor a treasure hunt in the hope that it would revive the sluggish program.

They worked very hard to ensure a successful event. Mark and Mary planned publicity and telephoned all youth members. Jeff and Jenny spent several hours planning and posting treasure-clues around the neighborhood. Jenny bought prizes to give to the winning team. Other adults were enlisted as drivers to transport carloads of exuberant teens to designated points.

A large crowd turned out for the treasure hunt. Everyone seemed to have a good time. There were enough memorable moments to spark laughter amongst teenagers and adults for a long time to come.

It sounds like the treasure hunt was a success, doesn't it? But a week later, Mark and Mary and Jeff and Jenny were feeling angry and resentful. Why? Because the following week, the activity planned was less appealing to the youth, and it failed to attract the same large number of young people.

The two sponsoring couples were disappointed. "Why did the kids have to be *entertained* every Sunday?" "Why weren't the parents more supportive?" "Didn't people realize how much effort they had expended on that treasure hunt?" "Didn't others understand that it was to be the *turning point* for the whole youth division?"

No.

Rescuing a floundering program is a big undertaking. There is seldom any one thing any of us can do to "fix" things. Lasting results come from asking those who are part of the program what needs to be done and how they might help make that happen.

The problem is more than unrealized expectations, like those of our frustrated foursome above. It also involves how we measure success--what goals we set for ourselves before we begin a project. If the two couples' criteria for success had included high attendance, willing participation, a mix of age groups, and a lot of fun, they would have judged the event as highly successful and celebrated it as it deserved. Instead, they felt deflated and ineffective. Why? Because the goal they set--revitalizing the youth program through a single event--was unrealistic. They tried to do the impossible and, naturally enough, they failed.

You can help volunteers achieve success by practicing realistic goal setting and establishing realistic steps to achieve your objectives. When volunteers are unclear about their purpose or when each has a different agenda, confusion results.

We sometimes lose sight of our mission completely. Consider the Vacation Bible School coordinator who hesitates to promote the popular summer event outside the church because she fears the program will be misused as a baby-sitting service. Of course it may be true about some families that 1) the parents will never visit the church, 2) the children won't bring any money for the offering and 3) there could be behavior problems. Still, *our purpose, and consequently our actions, should remain the same*, regardless of why a child might attend.

That's why it's so important to be clear about our goals. What do we want to happen as a result of our work? When our mission statement is a pervasive part of all our volunteer ministries, we learn to remind ourselves occasionally of our call as disciples. Why are we here? What are we about?

The same philosophy will prevent us from sabotaging our programs in other ways, as well. For instance, when those who serve regularly become a "clique" instead of a team, we create a hierarchy of "doers"--a select few who are in charge of all church activities. Recruiters and chairpeople who risk asking a wide variety of people to volunteer, rather than relying on "tried and true" friends all the time, will avoid that situation.

Lack of thought and care in scheduling church events can also sabotage our programs. I have occasionally found myself squirming to get out of attending a meeting or special event coordinated by a good friend. Although the friend may be asking for nothing but my presence, if I agree to all such requests, I find my calendar over-scheduled and my teeth on edge. There are other ways I can offer my support.

Finally, you may have noticed that some church events are thrown out like a gauntlet. As promoters, we may work ourselves nearly to death on some program we think the church *ought* to have. Then we wait to see just who the righteous are; who will take advantage of this "wonderful opportunity." In our own minds, we categorize those who attend as "good parents," "hard workers" or "supporters of the church." What we may be seeing instead are those who didn't have three other meetings that week, or those who managed to find a babysitter or even those who were fortunate enough to have time for dinner with their families before they came.

Attendance at church events can no longer be the sole determinant of who the faithful are. We will attract more participants, though, if we schedule judiciously, plan according to the needs and desires of the congregation, and enjoy the fellowship of those who can attend without judging those who cannot.

What Is Arbitrary Volunteerism?

Certainly a contradiction in terms, arbitrary volunteerism gives the appearance of involvement, but has little to do with willing participation. It sometimes occurs outside the areas of traditional volunteer service, but the effects carry over into all our programs.

This is what happens, for example, when we whisk the youth council off to visit residents of a nursing home without consulting the teens first. We do it when we pick someone from a congregation or classroom to read Scripture or liturgy aloud without getting their permission first. We do it by asking unsuspecting people to offer public prayer. We do it when we "elect" the only person absent from a meeting to do a job.

Without being aware of it, we may use service as an ostensible motive to accomplish other, ulterior goals. Have you ever scheduled the children's choir to sing during worship in order to bring back long-absent parents? Have you ever placed parents on a task rotation list because everybody has to take a turn preparing the youth suppers? Have you ever agreed to serve on a committee that "kept up with church expenses," only to find yourself embroiled in controversy over the use of church funds?

Me neither.

When we make folks uncomfortable, they stay home. Misrepresentation is a good reason to remain *un*involved.

Volunteering means choosing to give one's time for a specific purpose that furthers the church's mission and the volunteer's personal ministry. It is a means for developing self-confidence, not eroding it.

Two good rules of thumb are:

1. Never ask a captive audience to "perform."

2. If a person hasn't said "yes," the answer--for now--is "no."

How Can We Dismantle Barriers?

When we plan programs and structure jobs, we need to consider how our arrangements may impact others. It might not be a problem if we were all alike, observing identical cultural trends and living similar lifestyles. But that's not the case. (Anyway, that would be a club, not a church.) To be truly invitational, we must open our doors and our eyes to different ideas, customs and age groups.

Are there obstacles in your church which might prevent people who come from diverse educational, economic or ethnic origins from volunteering?

Single Adults/Single Parents

There is an erroneous assumption that unmarried adults must be grouped together for work, study and fellowship. Nonsense! Single adults make up a family unit, whether they have children or not. They enjoy being with a variety of people, just as we all do.

It's easier for single parents to accept volunteer responsibilities if the church provides child care. Family-centered projects that allow the children to participate are appealing. Consider trading services: find someone to transport Ann's daughter to the Girl Scout meeting and pick up her dry cleaning while Ann designs the lettering for the harvest bazaar flyer.

Single adults don't like labels that treat their singleness as an undesirable state. Neither do they appreciate being excluded from groups designated for "young couples" or "family fellowship."

Provide some volunteer opportunities that defy such restrictive classifications. Invite single adults to join the volleyball team, visit jail prisoners or teach Sunday School, just as you would any other adult.

The Unemployed

Do you know someone who has lost a job in the past 10 years? Corporate reorganizations, a fluctuating economy and budget cuts affect a tremendous number of people. Being unemployed is equally frightening for the executive or the clerk. The church can help.

Unemployed people can make excellent volunteers. For one thing, they need the network of relationships that volunteering can provide in the community. Many possess skills finely tuned by years of work experience. Volunteering is a legitimate way to keep one foot in the door of the business world while using special talents to help others.

Youth and Children

Young people volunteer for the same reasons you or I might. While consideration must be given to reading ability, attention spans, motor skills and family schedules, children are capable of working well together, or when paired with an adult. Teens are anxious for adult responsibility and appreciate our faith in what they can do. We must not make the mistake of planning *for* young people instead of *with* them!

What kinds of work do youth and children enjoy? Ask them! Here are some possibilities:

1. contributing artwork for display or for worship-bulletin covers
2. providing vocal and instrumental music for worship and fellowship
3. collecting aluminum cans for recycling
4. preparing dinner for senior adults
5. stuffing envelopes
6. designing flyers and newsletters

7. serving as greeters, ushers, acolytes and readers in the worship service
8. assisting with communion
9. visiting residents in nursing homes and shut-ins
10. creating banners
11. tutoring
12. picking up litter
13. corresponding with pen pals
14. planning special events (bike-a-thons, carnival booths, talent shows, etc.)
15. teaching younger children

In one community, children adopt senior adults as "grandparents." Every month, the two groups gather at the church for supper and socializing. The children prepare sandwiches (under the supervision of sponsoring volunteers) and serve the adults. The next month, the adults do the same for the children. Entertainment might be a game of "Go Fish," a sing-along, skits or a magic show. Everybody helps clean up, and everybody has a good time.

Jobs can be given to individual children, too. A child relishes "grown-up" work. Under the guidance of an adult, a child might paint wooden furniture for a Sunday School classroom or write a monthly column about children's division activities for the church newspaper.

Likewise, opportunities for teens should reflect their growing maturity levels. One church boasts a thriving program where youth receive training in child care, resulting in special certification. Some of these young people then work in the church nursery or offer their babysitting services to parents in the congregation. The church maintains a referral sheet, and staff members give glowing references for capable teenagers.

Many in this age group know how to work video equipment and operate computers better than their elders do. Some can drive, enabling them to deliver hot meals to the homebound. Others can take an engine apart and put it back together again. Teens serve as recreation directors, office assistants, lawn maintenance workers, music leaders and committee members. Teenagers provide any number of resources that allow our volunteer programs to shine.

New Families

It's hard to be new--in a classroom, on a job, in a church. Customary procedures are unfamiliar. Faces and names begin to blur after several introductions. Newcomers want to be friendly, but not appear overanxious. They need to fit in, but they're not sure where. Volunteering can help bridge the gap.

Some newcomers need an assimilating time before making a commitment. They will want to get to know people and experience how it feels to be a part of the organization. New members want to be invited, not pushed, to join in. Volunteering is not a prerequisite for church membership; we shouldn't treat it as such.

There are hearty individuals, however, who will plunge right into a volunteer job. Take Heather, for instance. Although new in town, she agreed to coordinate the July 4th family retreat for the church, even though she had not yet joined it. Because she had camping and group leadership skills, she felt qualified to attempt the project. Her ability to organize, delegate and plan caught everybody by surprise. The fact that she smiled throughout the preparations confused folks further! It turned out to be the best retreat in memory. The positive feedback from that experience was just the impetus Heather and her family needed. They joined the church and became active volunteers.

It's up to the volunteer director and/or clergy members to make an initial contact with visitors and new church members to determine how involved the family wishes to be with volunteering, and how soon. Volunteering is something we all want to do on our own terms. Be sure that potential volunteers know that their wishes and concerns are respected and that their service is always welcome.

Senior Adults

Senior adults today face more choices than ever before. Early retirement and the scattering of families allow greater freedom for many of them to travel, take college courses, pursue hobbies and volunteer. But for many, financial restrictions and lack of transportation may pose stumbling blocks to community activity. That's why it's important to offer volunteer opportunities for older adults that:

a) allow for occasional absence
b) include transportation options
c) pay expenses up front
d) require limited physical exertion
e) utilize teaching capabilities

Seniors bring professional and life skills to their volunteer work. You may have noticed that teenagers and children respond especially well to older adults. Seniors are survivors, and as such, they offer powerful handles to prison inmates, recovering batterers or child abusers, the terminally ill, the handicapped and the homeless. And they are often available during daytime hours--a virtue that is becoming increasingly rare.

Studies show that older adults exhibit less anxiety, a stronger will to live, greater social interaction and fewer aches and pains when involved in meaningful volunteer work. There is no such thing as being too old to volunteer.

Differing Ethnic and Economic Backgrounds

Have you ever been part of a volunteer group that decided to split project costs among themselves? If you were uncomfortable because you were a little short on cash, imagine the feelings of someone who simply doesn't have it in their budget to make that kind of contribution! It happens all the time, and we don't think about it.

For instance, Sunday School teachers are asked to attend a district training event, but the church doesn't pay the registration fee. Drivers are solicited for an out-of-town trip, but gasoline costs are not reimbursed. Sponsors for the community Easter egg hunt require each child to bring three dozen candy eggs.

Economic factors affect our volunteers and the programs they work in! It's important not to expect participants to donate money as a part of their volunteer service.

A generous mix of ages, races, cultures, personalities and economic backgrounds can only enrich our volunteer programs. Reach out, and invite people from neighboring churches and communities, as well as foreign visitors, to join your volunteer efforts.

Sponsor a tasting tea with dishes from many countries. Involve church members in student exchange programs. Ask persons from the Jewish community to assist volunteers in making a succoth for Thanksgiving. Donate volunteer hours to latch-key programs for children who come home from school to empty houses. Develop summer missionary projects to help those in poverty areas. Have a clothing drive for the local second-hand shop. Look for ways to foster acceptance and understanding through volunteer efforts.

How Can We Think "Celebration"?

We've examined our motives. We've broken down barriers. Now let's have fun! There is an element of joy in every ministry. Nourish your volunteer programs with good times.

Take a picture of the church secretary at the Youth Center with paint on her nose. Run humorous anecdotes about volunteers in the church newspaper. Name the church bus. Bring balloons to a planning session. Put job descriptions on colored paper. Use clip art to decorate letters and memos. Pick wildflowers for Sunday School teachers. Hug each other. Send notes of appreciation. Laugh.

The desire to serve is there. Volunteer programs that have integrity, are well managed and look like fun--those are the programs that attract people.

Motivate, accept, contribute, appreciate and celebrate; the cycle has begun. Keep it going!

Chapter Five

Recruitment and Recognition: Myths and Methods

Make it more fun to be on the inside participating than on the outside looking in.

Richard Steckel

For the Holy Spirit, God's gift, does not want you to be afraid of people, but to be wise and strong and to love them and enjoy being with them.

2 Timothy 1:7 (TLB)

Ask a group of church leaders what aspect of their jobs they like best. The odds are slim that anyone will stand up and joyously exclaim, "*Recruitment!*" Query the same crew about recognition of volunteers and you're sure to hear, "We have a lovely banquet once a year."

Because recruitment is such an exasperating problem for many of us, we view it as the rancher does the cattle prod--an unpleasant but necessary motivational tool. On the other hand, most of us *like* providing well-deserved recognition for volunteers, but we're not very imaginative about it.

Christian education and leadership magazines offer wonderful suggestions to aid in recruitment and recognition efforts...over and over again. The reason for the repetition is obvious--*need*. And the need for such reinforcement and helpful suggestions stems from the way we tend to separate recruitment and recognition from our overall volunteer management plan.

Or, sometimes recruitment and recognition *are* the plan. In either case, recruitment is precipitated by crisis and recognition tends to be perfunctory.

The overwhelming need to "get somebody to help" produces a distressing myopia that focuses all our energies on finding somebody--anybody--who will do the job.

And if you stop for a moment and think about recognition as the equivalent of a paycheck for employed workers, you can see that an annual event is not enough. Who can afford to work for twelve whole months without a dividend?

Crisis recruitment and inadequate recognition damage our programs and diminish our volunteers. We must find a way to transform both functions into integral parts of a natural, ongoing process in an efficient volunteer program. It can be done!

Why Doesn't the Recruitment Formula Work?

> Smile!
> Recruit in person.
> Define the job.
> Show related materials
> Explain training options.
> Follow up with a phone call.
> Say thank you!

Sound familiar? These steps make up the basic formula for recruiting volunteers. Why? Because, unlike Warren Salverson's Buffalo Bill Theory (where you lasso the one who is too slow to get away), this technique is courteous and civilized. It also occasionally produces positive results.

And it's better than the shorter version: "Here's the position. You'd be really good at it. Would you do it?"

The problem with any formula is that a) it must exist in a controlled, optimal environment to work and b) we are left without options when it doesn't. That's when frustration sets in. What's wrong with our congregation when they don't respond to THE FORMULA?

In fact, THE FORMULA is almost useless because it suffers from five basic flaws.

First, it is not supported by the groundwork of a solid volunteer management plan, one that allows us to fully evaluate the skills and interests of potential volunteers. Without such a plan, we become desperate "slot fillers," spending enormous amounts of time and labor trying to get people to say "yes." Even when we succeed, mismatched volunteers seldom invest themselves productively in work they care little about.

Second, the formula ignores individual gifts. We may think that a professional school teacher would like to teach Sunday School, but unless the Volunteer Coordinator has interviewed the prospect, we won't know that the teacher is also an expert carpenter who would relish the chance to refurbish homes for the elderly. Any time we define a job too rigidly, we risk stifling the creative flair a volunteer might contribute.

Third, this formulaic kind of recruitment is based on what the church needs. It assumes that a volunteer will say yes because, after all, we are the church. While service *is* an inherent part of our theology, ministry *can* take place at the local YMCA. Individuals volunteer for a variety of reasons. Altruism is only one of them. Until we know what people hope to get from their volunteer work, we can't very well assume that the first available job will be a meaningful one to them.

Which brings us to the fourth point. The formula specifies no benefits for the volunteer.

Department stores don't stay in business by insisting that it's their customers' duty to buy their products! Rather, they use advertising to demonstrate how their product will fill a need (real or imagined) for the prospective customer. Keeping that in mind, advertising is an excellent way to recruit. What's in it for the volunteer? An opportunity to make new friends? Learn a skill? Influence the system? Share special talents?

Make volunteering more attractive by offering a specific return to those who serve.

Finally, no formula will work until we remove some barriers. You may, for instance, be able to provide transportation, assist with child care, reimburse expenses, provide a substitute or allow more flexible hours. By offering more than verbal support, we make it easier to participate in volunteer ministries.

While the manner in which you ask for help is important, and your smile is certainly a plus, neither will bring lasting results without a support system that makes the volunteer as important as the job. Recruitment will always be a problem until we initiate efficient, professional management procedures.

The answer to many recruitment woes lies in the question: *What are you doing with the volunteers you have right now?* If current volunteers are feeling disgruntled and fatigued, the toothiest smile in the world won't entice anyone to join them.

On the other hand, if volunteer ministries are flourishing at your church, you can be sure that other members of the congregation will want to be part of the action.

Why Is It So Hard to Get Sunday School Teachers?

Let's look at a fictitious scenario illustrating the recruitment quandaries of one Sunday School superintendent. He is searching for a teacher for the fifth-grade class at Roadside Church.

Unsure where to begin, Mr. Superintendent pursues the obvious. He approaches professional teachers. By the time he's called half the teachers on his list, he gives up. A familiar chorus has given him second thoughts. It goes like this: "I'm with children all week. It's hard enough to make lesson plans for five days without having to prepare for Sunday too!"

Mr. Superintendent moves on to Plan B. He invites parents to teach. Most people work outside the home these days. Moms and dads, he thinks, would probably jump at the chance to spend more time with their children in Sunday School.

But listen to the response he gets: "I'm exhausted by the time the weekend finally gets here. I can't see myself coping with a roomful of fifth-graders on Sunday morning. Besides, I don't know enough about the Bible to teach it."

What about older adults? Mr. Superintendent figures that many are grandparents, and some seldom get to see their grandchildren. They are experienced and seem to love children. But the third and final plan also fails. "I took my turn teaching Sunday School when my own children were little. Now I want to enjoy being with my friends in the adult Sunday School class. Let the parents do their part."

Either the congregation at Roadside has a particular aversion to children, or the fifth-grade class has a terrible reputation! Or so it seems.

What may actually be the case, though, is that the structure of the program prohibits involvement.

How?

First, Mr. Superintendent was not given any information to help him identify persons who might *want* to teach Sunday School. The church had no means for discovering volunteer interests or talents. Left to his own devices, he began to make vast generalizations--about teachers, about parents and about grandparents. When his suppositions proved themselves false, he was ready to give up (as who wouldn't be?).

We could argue Mr. Superintendent's case by pointing out that plenty of professional teachers (parents, grandparents) do teach Sunday School. If he had simply continued down his list, he would eventually have found an agreeable party. But Mr. Superintendent was passed over for a promotion on his own job last week, he had to take his dog to the vet yesterday, and today, well, he just doesn't have that kind of staying power.

Now, he's so frustrated that he'll never agree to take the job as superintendent again. He may even resign before the year is out!

Do you recognize Mr. Superintendent? Do you see that simply by not knowing who potential volunteers are, we force ourselves to work with a handicap?

Let's see what other obstacles affect the recruitment efforts of Mr. Superintendent at Roadside Church.

The teaching term, it seems, is for a full year. Co-teaching, rotating teachers, or classroom aids are not options. There is no Children's Council, so teachers are expected to supervise class parties during holidays, plan mission projects and find their own substitutes, without benefit of a substitute-teaching team. They are also asked to keep the bulletin board outside the classroom decorated in a seasonal theme (although there are no supplies on hand).

And to top the situation off, the adult Sunday School classes don't include those who teach children in their fellowship activities, making them in effect, outcasts among their peers!

Now, regardless of the politeness of Mr. Superintendent's approach, or the delightfulness of his smile, would *you* want to teach at Roadside Church?

Probably not. Yet, you and I both can sympathize with poor Mr. Superintendent. We know his vision of the church is becoming clouded because what he sees is non-caring and lack of commitment on the part of those he approaches. We know. We've been there.

The error in Mr. Superintendent's approach is two-fold:

1) Because he has no job descriptions or clear expectations about what the job entails and because he provides no visible support system for the volunteer, everyone assumes the job he offers must be unattractive. And they're right.

2) He approaches recruiting on the basis of who can be trapped into doing the job, rather than on who really *wants* to do it or might be good at it.

Imagine the difference it would have made at Roadside Church if Mr. Superintendent had been able to invite a targeted group of people with skills and interests in teaching to make a commitment for a *quarterly* term, with a variety of *support services* and *resources*.

And suppose the pastor sent a personal note to Sunday School volunteers, recognizing their teaching gifts and acknowledging their contributions to Roadside's Christian education efforts. What if their pictures appeared in the church newsletter or their names in the worship bulletin? Don't you think Mr. Superintendent's odds would improve dramatically?

Why Don't Our Recruitment Methods Work?

Let's take a close look at some of the myths that continue to plague our recruitment efforts. Some of them, although alarmingly popular, can subtly undermine volunteer ministries.

MYTH # 1 *If you need someone to do a job, ask the busiest person you know.*

The theory that busy people are well-organized "go-getters" who will see that things get done isn't always true. Think how often you've heard a busy person complain, "I'm going in so many different directions, I feel as if I'm not doing anything very *well*." If we continue to recruit only the most active members of our church and community, we will succeed in wearing them out, while neglecting others with equally appropriate skills and a real desire to help.

MYTH # 2 *Only paid staff members need job descriptions.*

Without clear expectations that tie volunteer work to the church's mission and a common goal, committees are ineffective, programs flounder and volunteers lose interest. Job descriptions need not be rigid to provide direction and facilitate accomplishment. And remember--they make recruitment easier.

MYTH # 3 *If you intend to take advantage of a program, you have to assume your share of the responsibility.*

Do we really want to coerce a parent into supervising summer day camp activities just because his or her eight-year-old daughter wants to attend? There's a better way to secure competent, willing leaders.

MYTH # 4 *Ask your friends to help.*

While there's nothing wrong with inviting friends to participate, our ministry will be more complete if we continually look for ways to include a variety of people.

In instances where only friends gather, a dangerous precedent is set. Cliques and elite groups are contrary to the priesthood of all believers.

MYTH # 5 *Tell people there's nothing to the job and it really won't take much time.*

"The best for less" is not a slogan that lends itself to volunteer ministry. If there's truly nothing to the job, eliminate it. If we expect to maintain a quality program, we will develop high standards and work with our volunteers to achieve them.

Obstacles created by such myths exert a negative pressure on those already working in the program, as well as on those considering participation. Coercing people into jobs they have no interest in doing makes for a hollow victory. When we intimidate others into saying "yes" because they don't know how to say "no," nobody wins. The volunteer is unhappy. The program falters. And the recruiter blames the volunteer for not doing the job "correctly."

The mindset that "we must carry on at all costs" is unproductive. If we can't staff our programs, we need to look at the reasons why we can't. If the problems can't be corrected, it would be better to drastically change or even eliminate some programs altogether than to apply band-aids week after week.

What kinds of changes should you consider? Youth Coordinators of one congregation revamped the Sunday evening youth meeting format to dispense with having parents cook the traditional supper. They made the decision to do so because the number of volunteer cooks had declined for various reasons. Efforts to revitalize the enthusiasm of potential cooks failed. And it seemed the teenagers didn't care whether they had a meal prepared in the church kitchen, whether someone went out for hamburgers, or even whether supper was included on the evening's agenda at all.

Surprise! The youth program continued to be successful without prepared suppers.

What Are Some Logical Recruitment Steps?

When your volunteer ministries program is in good shape, recruitment ceases to be an overwhelming monster. Volunteer interests and skills are identified and recorded. Jobs are purposeful and clearly defined. Appropriate support and training are offered. Recognition is meaningful. Now you can recruit with confidence and enthusiasm!

Use whatever recruitment style fits your personality and your church. You may want to approach potential volunteers by telephone, by letter or by making a personal visit. One creative volunteer director sends mock telegrams announcing opportunities for service.

Be personal. Let people know why you are asking them to serve. Present the project or position realistically, explaining all pertinent information about the job. Include the following points:

> Project or job goal as it relates to mission
> Expectations/goal
> Time required/term of service
> Skills needed/training provided (if necessary)
> Support/resources
> Possible ways to achieve goals
> Accountability
> Opportunities for input/evaluation

When recruiting children or youth, remember to secure a parent's permission.

Any volunteer may want time to consider your proposal. Allow them to think it over for several days before calling again. See if they have unanswered questions or any reservations about the job. Whether the volunteer says "yes" or "no," follow up with a note or letter of thanks for accepting or considering the position. Confirm any details about the job.

You'll find a sample of what such a letter might look like on the next page.

What About Jobs that Are Hard to Fill?

If you see a pattern of rapid turnover in a job, or experience difficulty recruiting for a particular area, find out why and make some changes. Maybe the job is too complicated. Maybe it's boring or too restrictive. Perhaps the job needs to be tied in more closely with the church's mission statement or project goal. There may be personality conflicts between workers. Perhaps long and frequent meetings are discouraging participation.

If the problem is the job itself, redesign it. Write a new job description. Add a few perks. Divide the drudgery. Widen the scope of the job or, if it's too unwieldy, break it down into several jobs. Could the job be done at a different location? Explore different ways to achieve the desired results.

There's no rule that says, "Once a job is designed, it is forever more." The problem may be simply that the need that job once fulfilled no longer exists. Search out alternatives rather than trying to force people into jobs that are unattractive or don't fit.

How Can We Advertise Jobs?

Rely on a variety of recruitment methods to help enlist volunteers. Use the marketing and publicity suggestions from that chapter in this book. Develop an

Sample Thank-You Letter

Dear Jean,

I'm delighted that you will be a part of our volunteer team for the upcoming Fall Quarter. Your knowledge of animals and your willingness to share pets from your shop with nursing home residents will add a new dimension to our Elder Care program.

Mrs. Smith, the volunteer supervisor at Twin Oaks Nursing Center, has scheduled your visits for every Friday from 2:00 p.m. until 4:00 p.m. She will have a list of the residents' names and room numbers for you each week when you arrive.

We are having a name tag made for you to wear when you are on duty. I will call as soon as it is ready.

Thank you for donating your time and your skills. I look forward to visiting with you further about the project.

Sincerely,

Marie Jones,
Volunteer Coordinator

ongoing program that keeps church members informed about possibilities for involvement.

Occasionally, you might ask the pastor to announce a particular job-opening during the announcements of morning worship. You could run a weekly column in the church newsletter, or produce your own one-page newssheet as needed. Colorful posters attract attention. Schedule personal visits with potential volunteers. Keep recruitment needs in public and private prayers for your church and its ministries.

What Kinds of Recognition Are Meaningful?

Recognition does more than express appreciation. It validates. It motivates. It provides both incentive and visibility to the volunteer. It says to the volunteer that the work of individuals is important and that the church supports their effort.

Consultant Mike Murray often talks about the critical issue of "psychic pay" for volunteers. He stresses the need for volunteers to feel noticed, worthwhile, capable and powerful enough to make a decision.

Betty Stallings, president of Building Better Skills, in Pleasanton, California, lists the three "P's" of recognition: PERSONAL, POWERFUL, PLENTIFUL. She calls recognition "the art of letting someone know you noticed."

We have laughed about the annual banquet, but volunteers do deserve recognition for the work they do. What we must realize is that huge events may not be necessary or even desirable. The customary certificate or pin might be meaningful to some, but there are many, many ways to say thank you.

Rather than generic forms of appreciation, consider ways that will be most meaningful to individual volunteers. A corporate volunteer could benefit from a letter of commendation sent to the organization's president. A job-hunting volunteer could use documentation of his or her work for resume enhancement. A child would enjoy a badge inscribed "#1 Volunteer!" Sometimes, awarding positions of responsibility can show recognition of a job well done. Every gesture says, "We Care!"

Here's a list of ways to recognize volunteers. See if you can add TEN more!

^ Mention volunteers by name during worship and prayer

^ Greet volunteers warmly and ask them about their jobs

^ Supply a volunteer suggestion box

^ Issue a permanent, pin-on or clip-on name tag

^ Give a reception for volunteers, following the worship service

^ Invite volunteers to a staff planning session

^ Take time to listen to volunteers' problems

^ Send a donation to an overseas mission project in the volunteer's name

^ Be generous with well-deserved praise

^ Write a letter of recommendation for the volunteer's personnel file

^ Send birthday cards

^ Identify a "Volunteer of the Month"

^ Ask the pastor to write a personal thank-you letter

^ Reward innovation

^ Let volunteer leaders lead and volunteer workers work

Look for opportunities to tell volunteers their work is appreciated. Let them know you see both their actions and their caring. Praise the quality you see. Acknowledge a volunteer's capabilities in private conversations, during public gatherings of fellowship and worship and in writing.

Is there anyone who doesn't read a glowing letter of commendation more than once?

This kind of nurturing encourages a volunteer to stretch even further, to attempt new challenges. It not only promotes the volunteer program, it builds the volunteer.

Remember--when your program is flourishing, there's no annual gnashing of teeth. Both staff and lay leaders know that the best insurance against recruitment woes is happy volunteers. And the way to keep volunteers happy is to maintain a volunteer ministries program that enables people to do, or try or be whatever they choose.

Chapter Six:

Cultivating Leadership:
How to Help Volunteers Succeed

A leader is someone who dreams dreams and has visions; and can communicate those to others in such a way that they say "YES".
Michael F. Murray

And let us consider how we may spur one another on toward love and good deeds.
Hebrews 10:24 (NIV)

You know they're out there. Your congregation is full of intelligent, creative decision-makers. They are giving leadership to businesses, schools, government agencies, city councils, households and industries. Why aren't more of them holding positions of responsibility in the church?

My hunch is that since we are not known for efficiency, some of these potential leaders pass up church positions because of limitations on their time. Others, accustomed to decisive action, are put off by our cautiousness. And whether we want to admit it or not, a few simply don't find our church volunteer programs addressing the needs of the real world.

We have already discussed many ways to create more positive perceptions. By implementing needed changes in our volunteer programs, we can make service more relevant and hence more attractive. A vital step in this process is recognizing that we don't always have to *develop* leaders. We must begin to *identify* the leaders we already have. If our volunteer ministries are to strengthen and grow, we will find those leaders, solicit their help and then get out of the way and let them lead!

An exceptional leadership team strengthens every aspect of your volunteer ministries. That's why recruiting leaders through the Buffalo Bill theory (lasso the one that's too slow to get away) can be have such devastating results. The pastor cannot--and does not want--to have to keep checking up on volunteers. If the work of the church truly belongs to the laity, then we will see to it that our leaders are capable and responsible.

It's much easier to turn over the reins to a good manager than simply to pass the baton to the next runner and hope he or she goes in the right direction. That's what we've done in the past, with sometimes disastrous results.

Maybe that's part of the reason we guard our traditional way of doing things so carefully. It's safer. If we're unsure of our leaders, at least we can be sure about the "right" procedure.

But we needn't be afraid of strong leaders simply because they have a unique style or creative way of accomplishing things. We mustn't dismiss their approaches as too "business-like" or secular without giving them a chance to show what they can achieve.

We sometimes hear, "The church just can't be

run the way she runs her business. She doesn't understand that those principles don't work here."

Why don't they? Maybe because we haven't given them a chance. I'm not advocating the use of cutthroat tactics or indiscriminant wheeling and dealing. But until we allow strong leaders to enter our sanctum and wield their particular talents, we'll discourage all but the pillars from serving. And our pillars are getting tired of holding up the church!

We need the movers and shakers, the risk takers, the innovators if we are to remain fully functional and wonderfully alive! Without strong, capable leaders, we find ourselves all but paralyzed by careful maintenance: afraid to rock the boat, step on toes or move too fast. So we talk issues, file forms and table decisions.

Eventually, such lack of direction causes vision to fade and enthusiasm to wane. A ministry based on "just getting by" is no ministry at all.

Jesus' disciples possessed strong personalities. They didn't always agree. They sometimes went in different directions. But they were unified by a common purpose and a powerful love. The early church desperately needed exceptional leadership. We do, too.

How Can We Identify Leaders?

Don't rely on "professional packaging" when you're looking for capable leaders. They don't always wear three-piece suits.

You might be surprised to discover, for instance, that the young woman behind the camera at the local television station is also proficient in the use of sign language. Could she develop or supplement the program for your ministry to the hearing impaired? Or the garage mechanic, who knows what it means to start at the beginning and work through until a job is done--he might make a wonderful project director, able to overcome formidable obstacles to reach goals.

God uses those with quiet gifts as well as those with spectacular ones. Some leaders carry briefcases; others brandish hammers, diaper infants or build bridges. We need them all!

Your time-and-talent surveys, personal interviews and visits made by clergy and/or the volunteer director will provide a continuous flow of information about potential leadership in your church. The expertise is there. See how many ways you can find to reveal leadership talent. And then, provide the structure to support the newfound strength of your church.

What Can We Do to Encourage Leaders?

Job descriptions are helpful. Guidelines make sense. But insisting that leaders adhere to tradition like chewing gum to a shoe is counterproductive. Those with leadership abilities have good ideas and are generally capable of implementing them. We must allow them to move us in new directions.

Volunteer leaders should be given the authority to make decisions and the freedom to carry them out. We cannot put so many constraints on their actions that by the time they've been through the approval cycle, they have forgotten what they wanted to do in the first place. In the same sense, committees and project groups must have some degree of autonomy if they are to function effectively. People get excited about ideas they help cultivate. The resulting momentum brings excitement to the church.

Communication is essential if we are to coordinate efforts, share enthusiasm and relay information. Be creative in seeing to it that leaders know what's going on throughout the church. Duplicate efforts or confusion about who-is-doing-what will breed frustration and burned-out leaders.

Should Leaders Handle Tough Problems?

It has been noted that the first step toward solving a problem is to begin. In the church, we might revise that statement to say, "The first step toward solving a problem is to acknowledge that it exists!" It almost seems that somewhere in our Christian heritage somebody decided that we were always supposed to agree with each other--about everything--all the time. Good luck!

My experience shows that when we operate under the pretense that all is well when it isn't, the problems just get bigger. They may go underground, but they don't go away. We'll talk more about that in Chapter Eight, but it bears mentioning here because it directly affects volunteer leadership.

As a church, we must give our leaders *permission*, in an open and forthright manner, to deal with the problems that arise. Otherwise, their efforts are sabotaged and undercurrents flourish.

Suppose, for example, that the music committee decides to schedule the youth handbell choir to play during the worship service on the third Sunday of every month. Perhaps a parent raises objections because the family likes to go to visit Grandma on that Sunday. The chair of the music committee must be able to gather information, direct the discussion and make a reasonable and binding decision that will be in the best interest of all concerned.

If that decision is not respected, there is no need for the chair's presence/judgment/leadership in the first place!

Sometimes leaders have to make tough decisions. It goes with the territory. We help by participating, offering support and trusting the thinking behind the volunteer leader's decision.

We ought also not inhibit action by insisting that our leaders wait for a unanimous vote before making a move. Under such a constraint, leaders can be held hostage by a minority that's waiting for all the stars to be in alignment. It won't happen and we'll lose good leaders.

Leaders must be affirmed! We either have confidence in them or we don't (in which case, we should not place them in leadership positions). We don't have to create a hierarchy to give leaders a degree of authority. And we needn't assume that by granting them the power to make decisions and act on them, the church will fall into anarchy or autocratic rule.

Experienced leadership brings decisiveness and vitality to ministry.

Isn't It Important to Develop New Leaders?

While we want to utilize the "pros," we also want to develop potential in others with the desire and ability to *become* outstanding leaders.

Remember the first time someone exhibited enough confidence in you to get you started on a new endeavor? Whether you were six or thirty-six, the memory revives the good feeling of knowing that some one believed in you. Someone looked at you and saw potential. Chances are, you met or exceeded that person's expectations.

For many of us, the church provides a place to try on a new part of ourselves. There, we experiment with our abilities. We test the gifts God has given us. We learn, grow, follow and lead. The image of the church as a safe arena for *becoming* is both uplifting and theologically sound. What a joy to discover who we are and what we can contribute!

Some volunteers are more comfortable serving first as participants and then growing into leadership as they build experience and confidence. You can help foster a volunteer's potential by inviting workers to staff meetings, planning sessions or leadership retreats. Just as the business world provides continuing education for employees, the church will want to invest in the future of its volunteers.

For some, that means training. While it is wrong to insist that *all* volunteers need training, it is equally misguided to assume that *none* do. Common sense dictates which volunteers fall into which group.

Imagine how offensive it would be to physicians to require their attendance at first-aid training for camp counselors. (They might lead such sessions, though.) And while a workshop session called "Introduction to Elementary Curriculum Studies" could be helpful to new teachers, an experienced Sunday School teacher may resent being required to participate.

Training can be a helpful tool for improving skills or acquainting volunteers with a new job. It should open doors and boost confidence, not impart dictums about how a job should be done.

What kinds of training do your volunteers and potential volunteers need? Ask them.

Do Workshops Work?

Those of us with responsibilities for managing volunteers tend to look to the public schools as models for training. We decide to hold a workshop using the traditional classroom format. We line up chairs, bring in a chalkboard, call in an expert and announce to our volunteers that they *should* come.

Often, it doesn't work. For one thing, we're not in the third grade any more. Adults learn differently from children. We bring a substantial amount of skill and experience to whatever job we pursue. We have definite ideas about how we see ourselves in a volunteer role. We would rather have input into the design of a program than be lectured about what we are to do.

This is not to say workshops are never effective. Far from it! I can leave a well-planned, top-notch training session feeling as if I could do anything! But when the event is of poor quality, I find myself wondering why I didn't stay home to change the oil in the car or chase dust bunnies from behind the refrigerator.

Once you've been to a snoozer, it's hard to get excited about attending another one. One of the volunteer director's responsibilities is to spot outstanding seminar opportunities and pass the information along. Watch for clues that point to quality, such as a promotional brochure that describes a well-designed event and lists the leaders and their qualifications. If you're unsure, call someone connected with the workshop and ask for more information or references.

When you are reasonably convinced about a workshop's merit, the next question is usually: "How do we get volunteers to go?"

If the workshop provides information that volunteers *want*, if the church encourages attendance through publicity and one-on-one contacts and if assistance is offered, many volunteers will gladly attend.

Offer support and recognition to those who choose to participate. Try these measures to encourage attendance:

1. Send a letter to the volunteer under the pastor's signature, along with brochures or promotional materials.
2. Publicize the names of all who register in your church newspaper.
3. Offer participants a forum in which to share what they have learned once they return.
4. Provide child care.
5. Offer the church bus or van for transportation.

6. Notify volunteers whether the church will pay for all or part of the registration fee.
7. Photograph participants at the workshop and display the pictures on a bulletin board or in the newspaper.
8. Acknowledge volunteers' outstanding commitment in a letter, phone call or personal visit.

What Are Some Other Training Options?

There are more training options now than ever before. We needn't lecture, threaten, bore or inconvenience a volunteer who wants to learn something new. Churches are using community education classes, slide shows, video presentations, university extension courses, apprenticeships, guided tours and field trips, resource books, mentor programs and panel discussions to help train volunteers.

Link your training efforts with those already in progress in your area. Find out what city and government agencies offer. Inquire about pooling resources and sharing expertise.

The possibilities are endless. Imagine the benefits of quality training to help volunteers conduct interviews, learn the basics of storytelling or use computer software to produce church newsletters.

Sometimes the offer to provide training will bring new volunteers into service. For example, one church revived interest in the annual bazaar by hosting sessions to teach volunteer workers how to make a variety of craft items, from earrings to intricate needlepoint designs. People of all ages contributed their newly-developed skills, making the bazaar a success and learning enjoyable hobbies in the process.

Good training opportunities are those that are well done, efficient and relevant to the volunteer's job.

And remember--training that brings about no change is as effective as a parachute that opens on the first bounce.

Whether your volunteers require extensive training or merely a brief orientation, keep in mind that the purpose is to help them succeed. Volunteers have the right to be informed about what it is they are expected to do, as well as the option of deciding whether they need help doing it.

How Can We Support Volunteer Leaders?

Our congregational members are our greatest resource. Their fresh ideas foster a brighter vision. Their participation--as volunteer support staff or as leaders--is essential if we are to recognize our potential as a loving church. What kinds of support do we offer those who want to help? How often do we thank our leaders for the jobs they do? Do we respect their decisions? Can we offer a wider range of training choices?

Your volunteer program will provide opportunities to serve and chances to rest. All jobs will be important. All ideas will be heard. Take the risk of allowing individual differences and outstanding leadership. Help create a climate that permits challenge and renewal. Grow disciples.

Chapter Seven

Marketing: Unless You Want to Keep Your Church a Secret

Everything about an organization talks.
Philip Kotler

Let your light shine before others, that they may see your good deeds and praise your father in heaven.
Matthew 5:16 (NIV)

My house boasts a wonderful front porch. A swing hangs from the rafters--strategically placed for optimum shade and the best view. I seldom luxuriate there. Not because of an allergy to bee stings or an aversion to the hot Texas sun, but because I allow my hectic lifestyle to rob me of that pleasure. Nobody who wishes that grocery carts came equipped with blaring horns is going to tarry any length of time in a porch swing.

Once upon a time, when conversation was commonplace, families gathered on porches or in parlors during twilight hours. They also grew their own food, hung their clothes out to dry, went to church every

Sunday and "did the right thing" as a matter of course. No doubt, some of us still do some of these things some of the time. But our living patterns are different; our world is more complicated and diverse than the world our parents and grandparents lived in. Instead of adhering to tradition, we forge our own paths.

Did you know that denominational loyalty is almost extinct today?

Did you know that congregations are growing older? That the numbers of the unchurched increase daily? That people who are "shopping" for a church search actively for specifics, such as relevance to their daily lives, programs that meet secular as well as spiritual needs, and a place of rest and replenishment?

What a challenge! The church has a powerful mission to fulfill. Our volunteer ministries form an integral part of that mission. We can continue to write our message on scrolls if we like. But if we're serious about church growth--about reaching our unknown neighbors, building faith-to-life connections and affirming individual gifts through service--then we'll explore marketing options that get results in *today's* world.

Some readers will argue that "we shouldn't have to promote ourselves." Perhaps. But if we're going to move in new directions and open ourselves to God's possibilities, we may have to set aside some of our "shoulds" and "shouldn'ts."

Statements like, "Our members should read the church newspaper," or, "So-and-so should do more to help the less fortunate" really serve only to trap us within our own expectations. Besides, "shoulds" seldom motivate the unchurched, the disillusioned, the exhausted or the sinner.

In this chapter, we'll look at various ways you can use marketing techniques to proclaim your message. "Marketing" is how we tell others who we are, affirm for them who they are and rejoice together in who God is.

Why Publicize?

You want not only the community but the members of your own church to know what's going on! We sometimes take it for granted that the congregation is well informed. Yet, how many times have you heard, "I would have been there, but I didn't know about it"?

Your in-house and community-wide publicity efforts serve to inform and educate, as well as to invite participation. They convey a style--a climate that can attract visitors and create a positive image. Marketing will also keep your church competitive in a time when all of us are bombarded with choices every Sunday morning and throughout the week.

Your publicity campaign will help you enlist volunteers, gather civic support and even increase contributions. By using publicity garnering methods that are free or inexpensive, you achieve a high return for the time and money you put into them.

In her book, *Marketing Magic for Volunteer Programs*, Sue Vineyard says that by assuming a marketing outlook we are "identifying real, current needs and adapting programs and services to respond to those needs." This is the kind of relevance that today's volunteer (and potential church member) is looking for. When we draw attention to our ministries, we invite interest and participation.

You've done it. Remember the time you posted the revival notice in the window of the local grocery store? Maybe you invited a reporter to a Thanksgiving feast your church sponsored for the indigent. There's nothing decadent about using good promotional practices for your church's programs.

In fact, the bestselling business book, *Megatrends 2000*, quotes Jack Sims, a former pastor and religious consultant in Placentia, California, as saying, "Churches must adapt and have a marketing orientation if they are going to attract baby boomers. I think that if the churches adopt three simple changes, 5 to 10 million baby boomers would be back in the fold in one month." The changes Sims advocates are advertising, emphasizing product benefits (such as nursery schools or social groups) and practicing good customer relations--being nice to people.

It sounds simple! But it takes determination, commitment and a productive publicity plan.

How Do We Develop a Good Publicity Plan?

You know what a difference an effective Evangelism Committee makes. Imagine the results if their efforts, along with the work of other programs and projects, were supported, encouraged and enlarged by appropriate publicity.

There are people in your congregation who can help. They are the journalists, public relations representatives, television and radio station employees and photographers in your community. Form a Publicity Committee and make them part of it. Have every commission or group project name someone to report to it.

Then, decide who your target audience is and how you will reach them.

We often make the mistake of attempting to cover too much at one time. A good publicity plan will encompass activities throughout the year, but it will use specially designed tactics to appeal to specific target groups. For instance, if you want to recruit retired seamstresses to make cloth bears for the crisis center, you won't advertise for them on the local rock radio station. Nor will you depend on a press release to the local newspaper to solicit teenagers for a Big Brother/Big Sister mentor program.

Your Publicity Committee will include both

direct and indirect measures for gaining coverage. Direct methods let you go straight to the public with posters, handouts or billboards. Indirect methods entail some form of personal contact with the people who put out the news, such as newspaper or television editors and reporters. You can decide whether to contact them in person, by mail or over the phone, but if you know you will be dealing with a single editor on an ongoing basis, sooner or later, you will want to visit the office and introduce yourself. Journalists, like most other human beings, respond better to names they can associate with faces and a warm handshake.

Be sure to keep the records on your media contacts updated. A letter addressed to an editor who's been gone three years doesn't create the best impression.

Radio and television stations are required by law to devote a certain amount of air time to public service announcements. Take advantage of these free "advertising opportunities" by sending them brief news releases addressed to "PSA Director."

Public Service Announcements should contain only the essentials: who, what, where, when and, if applicable, how much? They should also include an invitation, a word or two that clearly invites the public to attend, even if it's only "Y'all come!" You'll find an example of a PSA with the other examples at the end of this chapter.

If the cause you are promoting is of widespread public interest, contact a local speaker's bureau and let them know that you have people available who can speak knowledgeably on the subject.

It's easier to obtain the kind of publicity you want if you understand the peculiarities of the media. One radio executive claims to throw away 80%-90% of the press releases he receives each day. Why? Maybe because the information is not truly newsworthy. Or because it arrived after the fact or too late for him to act on. Perhaps it wasn't relevant to his particular audience. Or a major news event "bumped" stories of less urgency.

You can beat the odds of having your news releases "trashed" by following some basic guidelines.

1. Remember--news is a perishable commodity! Chuck Wolf of Wolf Media Consultants says, "Think of news like guacamole dip. It's only palatable when it's fresh!"

2. News means tutti-frutti on a vanilla day. Put a creative edge on your efforts. Make the information seem exciting and unique.

3. News must serve a purpose. How could your material be more informative or offer additional solutions to a problem?

4. News must be relevant. It's not enough to make a report. You must also make people care.

5. News is an invitation to action. What do you want your readers or listeners to *do* as a result of your spiel?

Tie projects and programs to issues listed as high priorities in the FCC Ascertainment Survey. Get a copy from the Public Affairs Director of your local radio and television stations. Published once a quarter, the list classifies "Hot" issues within a community, such as the economy, education, crime, drug abuse or race relations.

Contact the media if your church has a successful program related to any of the subjects listed in the Survey. Offer different perspectives on the issue from the pastor, the volunteer coordinator and a volunteer worker.

Watch for "photo opportunities" and make the most of them.

Especially inviting to the media are projects that link church and community. The example beginning on page 109 shows how a church in Houston, Texas linked up with the YMCA and a local radio station to promote a major event.

More and more businesses are willing to contribute money and time to assist worthwhile causes these days, so remind your Publicity Committee of the possibility of recruiting professionals to volunteer their services. Ask an advertising executive if one of her graphic artists might design a project logo. Check out the possibility of having your brochure printed free at the print shop next door to the church. Invite the mayor to blow the starting whistle for the walk-a-thon. Solicit a local veterinarian to judge the dog show (with proceeds going to the animal shelter).

Help like this will not only put a professional polish on your efforts, it will attract attention and further the community spirit that bonds businesses, churches and communities. (Be sure to write thank you letters. And give credit where credit is due.)

In the past, we've known it was not in our funds to buy publicity. We've not worked very hard to enlist outside help. Consequently, we've missed some golden opportunities. These days, church-growth experts recommend allocating 5% of the total church budget to publicity. As someone's wise grandmother once said, "Stopping at third base adds nothing to the score." Go for it!

What Methods Provide the Best Publicity?

Think of promotion as "letting your light shine." The methods discussed below vary in the cost and effort required. Let the means reflect the event. Go all out for monumental occasions. Try different approaches. Keep your goal in mind. And TARGET!

The Press Release

These are short (1 to 2 pages) chronicles that list the WHO, WHAT, WHEN, WHERE and WHY of your story. Type them double-spaced on your church letterhead. Include the names, addresses and telephone numbers of at least two people to contact for further information.

Put your most important news in the first sentence. (Editing at the newspaper office is often done from the bottom up. You know what's essential, but the editor may not.)

Include quotations from people involved in the project, if possible.

Signify the end of your release by centering "30" at the bottom of the last page.

Mail the release two weeks in advance to a specific editor, by name. If you don't know the name of the editor, call the newspaper office and ask whoever answers the phone. Get them to spell it.

Politely request a specific date (or range of dates) for publication.

Follow up with a phone call to answer questions or clarify information for the editor.

You'll find an example of an effective news release with the other examples at the end of this chapter.

The News Conference

Save this for the biggies! Provide media with a press kit, and be prepared to field a variety of questions. Plan your timing carefully. Check the futures file at news outlets to avoid problems with scheduling. You don't want your editor to be off covering a social event at the hour you set for your conference. Be sure there are plenty of chairs in the room where the conference will be held, see that the microphone works, keep the speakers brief and provide light refreshments. Thank reporters for coming and send notes of appreciation for coverage.

The Feature Story

These are usually written by a reporter on the media staff. Be sure the subject of the story is a good interviewee--reasonably articulate and poised. Feature stories must have a high human-interest value. Supply enough background information to engage the reader or audience on several levels. Suggest photo opportunities for stills. Rehearse good "spontaneous" quotes.

Newspaper Display Ads

Display ads can be excellent attention-getters, but they can also be expensive. You'll pay by the column inch, so keep your announcements clear, simple and uncluttered. Artwork adds pizzazz. Don't forget the date, time and place. Most newspapers have a design expert on staff who can help you lay out the ad.

Public Service Announcements

Available in 10, 20, 30 or 60 second segments, radio spots can be either taped or broadcast live. Some cable television stations will run PSAs in printed form on a community access channel. Use these to invite the public to a special event or to announce the beginning of a specific campaign or project. Include the church's phone number. This service is provided free in most areas.

Radio and TV Talk Shows

Most local radio and television stations host talk shows and are always on the lookout for timely topics and interesting guests. Some shows are taped; others are live. Even if the show airs at 5:00 a.m., you can still use the exposure, no matter how limited. Contact the station manager or talk show producer if you feel that your latest project or mission warrants attention. Remember to keep up with the Ascertainment listings and draw direct correlations between your church's volunteer efforts and subjects of major interest in the community.

If you are scheduled for a talk show, supply the interviewer with a list of possible points to discuss. Arrive early to snatch a few minutes with the host before the program for a handshake and a friendly smile. If the talk show includes "call-ins" from the public, have some well-prepared callers ready to dial with pertinent questions you want answered. (It's not cheating; it's good planning.)

Find a thespian--or at least a bona fide "ham"--in your congregation to provide showmanship and vital information.

Video Presentations/Slide Shows

With the advent of home video equipment, visual displays are easier than ever. Quality, however, is another matter. Your production won't look "Hollywood" unless you have the money or expertise to provide the polish. Even without it (depending on your purpose), you can make quite satisfactory presentations to help viewers "see" the results of volunteer efforts, project accomplishments and monetary contributions.

Show faces, not places. Convince your audience

that your project can and does make a difference in people's lives.

There are many components to a successful video program. You will need a team to write the script, choreograph the players, find the best locations, arrange for sound effects or music and design any graphics you may want. I understand that there are people in the world who consistently remember to take the lens cap off their cameras before they shoot. These are the folks you want to recruit for help with this one.

Newsletters

Use a marketing slant when designing a newsletter for your volunteer projects. "Sell" the value of what you are doing. Leave the birthdays for your in-house communications, and provide news, photographs and recruitment incentives in a product you photocopy or complete on your desktop publishing system.

Photos copy better if you have a velox made first at the print shop.

Make the newsletter eyecatching and concise. Use colored paper, clip art and effective headlines. Keep it newsy.

Send copies to volunteers, local libraries, businesses, media representatives and community service agencies.

Use a warm, friendly style, and you will not only increase awareness of your volunteer ministries, you will find yourself with more volunteers.

Booklets and Brochures

An attractive booklet describing your church's programs and volunteer opportunities is a wonderful resource for new and established church members. It's also a handy tool to include in press kits and distribute to libraries or community service fairs. Let your creativity and versatility show.

The brochure need not be elaborate or expensive, but it should project your church's image as a leader in volunteer ministries. If you work with a local printer, you can often get superbly professional help with design and artwork.

You'll find an example of an effective brochure at the end of this chapter.

The Yellow Pages

Many churches find attractive Yellow Pages ads an effective way to "introduce" the church to people looking for a place to worship. Don't forget to list the times of your services and your program options and to indicate that you have a viable volunteer ministries program. That may be just the impetus to bring a new face into your midst.

Bulletin Boards

Don't underestimate the recruiting power of well-designed bulletin boards. Use them in the church and in the community. Do more than decorate. Inform. Invite. I hear some of you groaning. Believe me, there are folks in your congregation who *love* to do bulletin boards. Find them. Your surveys and interviews will help.

Encourage them to use more than construction paper and ready-made letters. Let them turn the display boards into works of art with fabric, craft materials, elements from nature, drawings and photographs. It's one more way to communicate your caring spirit and your commitment to volunteerism.

What Can We Do to Establish Good Public Relations?

Remember that newspeople don't often get their stories by osmosis. You have to help. If you are well-prepared and efficient in your approach, they will not only seriously consider your proposal, they will like you!

Don't contact the press every time a volunteer sneezes, but do approach them with newsworthy items. Put a different twist on a familiar story, or find a new solution to some tough problems.

And remember that you're only one of the many individuals and organizations vying for the attention of the media. If the story you propose is not a piece they can use, accept their decision graciously and try again later.

One year not long ago, the trend in Vacation Bible Schools was to release helium-filled balloons with messages inside. The local paper photographed one church's balloon release and was plagued the rest of the summer by calls from other churches wanting coverage of their balloon extravaganzas.

"It was news the first time," the beleaguered reporter said, "but we couldn't run a balloon picture every week!"

Even if your event is better, more spectacular or more dynamic, know that if it's been done before, it's not likely to merit media coverage. Have a good time, anyway.

Part of maintaining and directing a volunteer program is a flair for fostering relationships--with volunteers, community leaders and members of the media. Take time to say hello and try to remember names. Send thank-you notes. The more visible your ministries are, the more effective you can become. People see the need, are inspired by others and join forces.

Remember, ultimately, there is no better advertising for your volunteer program than a satisfied volunteer and none worse than a dissatisfied one. As managers of volunteer programs, it is essential that we take care of the people who take care of our projects. Part of letting our light shine is permitting others to see, and become involved in, our ministries. It's not just good public relations. It's sound theology.

Linking Church, Community and Media

Thanks to Chuck Wolf, News Director at KIKK AM and FM in Houston, Texas, for these excerpts from a letter showing media sponsorship of a church event/community event.

... KIKK will be happy to work with the Hands Helping Houston project of the Downtown Y and the First United Methodist Church. We will promote the event (on these dates) with five :30 produced promos and 15 :10 live promos. All day Friday, March 25, KIKK's Harvey T. will be there with his KIKK Van to provide music and/or PA capabilities, along with the presence of our 20' inflatable KIKK boot.

In return for KIKK's promotion, we understand we will receive the following:

Feature mention in the 13,000 circulation United Methodist Reporter and the 7,000 circulation Downtown Y Fitness Facts.

Mention in press releases, fact sheets, event day literature, flyers and other promotional literature.

As a major event sponsor, we also expect to be included in Channel 13's editorial support mentioned in your letter.

We'll also be acknowledged as a sponsor on the Golf Tournament connected with "Hands," as well as at the celebrity dinner and auction, and at the auctions on Saturday.

We understand that we will receive 4 complimentary tickets to participate in the May 10 Golf Tournament.

As you know, "Hands" qualifies for PSA announcements. Please send a fact sheet on the event ASAP so we can schedule some time. Contact us, too, for any interview possibilities....

Sincerely,

Note: ...if the above conditions meet your approval, please sign and return to me a copy of this letter.

Signature

Agreed:_____

Date:_____

Sample Press Release

FOR: Anytown News Gazette
FROM: Elm Street Church
        3517 Elm Street
        Anytown, Anystate 90101

CONTACT: Sally Jones, Volunteer Coordinator
          843-9329

DATE: March 4, 1992

FOR IMMEDIATE RELEASE

Zoo Volunteers to Be Honored

The public is invited to a special celebration recognizing 25 volunteers from the Elm Street Church Discipleship program on March 15 from 3-5 p.m. in the Gazebo Garden at Anytown Zoo. In case of rain, the event will move to the auditorium in the Planetarium Center.

The Local Yokel band will provide music throughout the afternoon. Other activities include a petting zoo, tours of the newly opened primate facility and information booths highlighting the zoo volunteer programs. Visitors will receive free balloons and refreshments.

The Reverend Scott McClain, senior pastor at Elm Street Church, will present certificates during the volunteer recognition ceremony at 3:30 p.m. Top honors of the year will go to Mabel

-more-

Smith and Bob Cartell. Each logged over 400 volunteer hours at the zoo last year.

About her work, Mabel said, "I've always liked animals, and as a former teacher, I knew I could teach children. The training the zoo provided was excellent preparation for my role as education coordinator. Being here isn't work. It's just plain fun!"

The zoo program is only one of many volunteer opportunities provided by the church's Discipleship program. You can find out more about volunteering by calling Elm Street Church at 843-9329.

-30-

Sample Public Service Announcement

News from the Volunteer Program
Elm Street Church, Anytown, Anystate 90101

Contact: Sally Jones, Volunteer Coordinator
843-9329

Date: June 1, 1992

<u>For</u> <u>Immediate</u> <u>Release</u>

FREE FISHING DERBY FOR KIDS

20 Second Spot

ANNOUNCER: Kids 4 to 16! Get ready for a fun-filled day of fishing competition during National Fishing Week. Volunteers from Elm Street Church are holding a FREE fishing derby just for you on Saturday June 9.

There'll be prizes in four age categories, tips from fishing experts, refreshments, and a casting contest, besides lots and lots of fishing.

You have to be registered to participate, and you'll need to bring a parent or guardian with you on the 9th. To find out how to register and get in on the fun and prizes, call Elm Street Church at 843-9329 any day between 9 a.m. and 5 p.m.

-end-

Sample Brochure

Sample Booklet Page, Reprinted with permission from St. John Lutheran Church in Winter Park, Florida.

Group Song Leader

IMPORTANCE TO OUR CHURCH: Music is a vital part of many of our learning experiences at St. John. A strong song leader is essential.

JOB DESCRIPTION: Song leader will prepare music appropriate for the event and lead the group in singing.

TIME FRAME: Song leaders are needed several times during the year. Commitments would be for one event at a time.

SKILLS TO BE USED/DEVELOPED: Musical ability and ability to feel comfortable leading groups in singing.

NUMBER OF VOLUNTEERS: We can use approximately ten volunteers per year.

TRAINING REQUIRED: Song leaders will be given information about each event and the type of music required.

BENEFIT FOR THE VOLUNTEER: Those who enjoy singing will enjoy sharing music with others in the St. John family.

Sample Brochure

The Volunteerism Committee of Our Saviour's Lutheran Church in Merrill, Wisconsin, agreed to share their powerful statement about volunteers in the church.

VOLUNTEERS IN CHRIST
MISSION STATEMENT

"Our mission is to worship, to learn, to witness, and to serve God by focusing all of our resources on those activities which bring people into the family of God until all are one in Christ."

FOREWORD

Giving of our gifts of time and talent as well as our financial resources in the support and service of the Lord is one of the most soul-satisfying results of volunteering to participate in church activities.

To aid volunteers in having more satisfying experiences by knowing what committee work will entail, the volunteerism committee has prepared this handbook of mini-descriptions of the multitude of volunteer opportunities in the church. The purpose is to open the doors to every member who has a desire to be involved.

The Volunteer Coordinator and committee has more detailed position descriptions available for those activities and committees you are interested in. The Volunteer Coordinator also puts you in touch with people who have responsibility in your area of interest.

The Pastors, Church Secretary or information in newsletters and bulletins will put you in touch with the Volunteer Coordinator.

IDENTITY STATEMENT

"Our Saviour's Lutheran Church is a body of believers in Christ blessed by God through baptism seeking to serve God and expand His kingdom by making use of our individual talents and gifts."

Sample Brochure

St. Aidan's Episcopal Church in Boulder, Colorado, uses a different format to convey information about the church and its volunteer ministries. Below is an artist's drawing of their information and activities brochure. The actual measurements are 14 and 1/2" by 6".

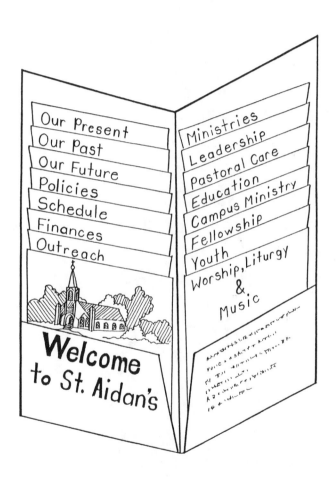

Sample Poster

Thanks to West Side Presbyterian Church, Ridgewood, New Jersey.

Each one as a good manager of god's different gifts must use for the good of others the special gifts he has received from god

I Peter 4:10

Sample Flyer
"Sharing Our Success II," by Diane Richardson.

Chapter Eight

Committees that Count: Make Your Meetings Matter

Nothing makes people stay away from volunteer work like attending meetings with little or no purpose.
                                        Douglas W. Johnson

So we, though many, are one body in Christ, and individually members, one of another.
                                        Romans 12:5 (RSV)

Why are we here?

Do you find yourself sitting through aimless church committee meetings, your mind wandering and your fingers drumming? One of the major obstacles to volunteer involvement is the church's penchant for meetings. Our structure may actually impede our effectiveness!

You know the familiar refrain: If this is the first Tuesday, it must be meeting night. Why? Because we *always* meet on the first Tuesday of every month. Why? Because we've always done it that way.

STOP! The costs are too high--costs in staff time, utilities, nursery care, and yes, coffee. More important--costs in volunteer energy, thought, time and inconvenience. We simply cannot afford the costs of unproductive meetings.

Eavesdrop on a group of volunteer administrators as they listed their pet peeves at a recent seminar at the University of Colorado:

~ meeting for "no reason"

~ too much "socializing"

~ getting off track

~ unprepared chair or committee members

~ one person monopolizing the meeting

~ people dropping in and out of the meeting

~ staff/volunteer power struggles

~ distracting whispers and talking

~ "railroaded" decisions

~ having to take minutes

~ not starting or stopping on time

"We don't ever DO anything!" they said. "We make elaborate plans that never get carried out."

Volunteers need to feel that their presence matters--that what they discuss and plan will result in decisive action and visible ministry.

When you and I attend meetings, we expect to

accomplish something. Let's look at some of the factors that interfere with effectiveness.

What's Wrong with the Reporting Mode?

"I never knew why I was asked to serve on the Evangelism Committee," one volunteer said. "I showed up for almost all the meetings, but nobody asked me for my opinion about anything, I wasn't given a specific job to do, and it seemed like all I did was listen to reports from staff members and group leaders. I wish they had sent me a memo, instead!"

Committees that are stuck in a reporting mode are so busy hearing where they've been that they can't decide where they're going. It's after-the-fact management. It's dull and it doesn't invite volunteer participation.

Terry, for instance, served as program director on the staff of a large suburban church. Every Tuesday afternoon, the staff met to report on the past week's activities and on upcoming events. Every Tuesday. Besides the weekly meeting, a myriad of committee meetings scattered throughout the month required Terry's presence. Again and again, she summarized, revised and presented her reports.

Terry's church relied heavily on its staff for direction and program maintenance. So she was caught between reporting on volunteer activities and leaving room for input from her volunteers. The delicate balance was difficult to maintain.

Terry noticed that attendance at some of the meetings began to decline. Eventually, nobody came except staff members and committee chairs. They spent the time making the same reports to each other that they'd heard before and probably would hear again,

What happened to kill the effectiveness of these meetings? Terry knows. "We were using our meeting time," she says, "to report rather than to explore goals, make decisions and determine action. The sessions became overburdened with staff, which took leadership away from the volunteers. Naturally enough, they just slipped away."

As Terry's experience illustrates, when nothing is required of volunteers except their presence, they feel unnecessary. They become an audience rather than a committee. Their attention strays, and their physical presence soon follows it.

Effective meetings need pertinent agendas and capable chairpersons, but not necessarily clergy or staff members. Unless church professionals have a direct role in a volunteer project or committee function, there are better ways for them to lend support than by always being present.

Breaking out of the reporting mode requires that whoever chairs the meeting accept responsibility for the agenda. That includes making sure that the committee members know what the issues are, because even a meeting held for the purpose of discussion must move the group in the direction of their goals.

If no action at all is required of committee members, the chair must decide whether the meeting is necessary and call it off or postpone it if it's not.

To increase the effectiveness of your meetings, try skipping the reports. Try dealing with a clear agenda, making critical decisions and taking action. Let volunteers know that their opinions do matter. Wake everybody up and give them the chance to participate.

How Can We Combine Business and Fellowship?

Volunteers join committees and attend meetings for different reasons. Donna likes the chance to be with friends and talk about church matters. Frank wants to work on those projects that produce immediate and visible results. Kay likes the feeling of being in charge of what happens.

If Donna, Frank and Kay are on the same committee, they may all arrive at a meeting with vastly different expectations. One needs to feel comfortable, with time for chatting and coffee. One requires an action agenda, resulting in specific responsibilities for each member. One welcomes the opportunity to influence the system--to utilize leadership skills.

All these expectations are legitimate to committee interaction. The challenge is to prepare and conduct our meetings so that individuals can function well enough to reach committee goals, and be comfortable at the same time.

Allow for a combination of geniality and purposefulness. Try serving coffee in the fifteen minutes before the meeting. At the appointed time, bring the committee firmly to order. Set a friendly tone and briefly outline the agenda. Be flexible within reason, but don't allow meandering or grandstanding.

Suggest that peripheral matters be taken care of outside of meeting time. Ask members for their opinions and take everyone's feelings into consideration. Conclude on time. Thank participants for coming.

It takes an astute and intuitive leader to conduct satisfactory meetings--a major factor in any committee's success.

What Makes a Good Committee Chair?

For those new to the job, chairing a committee can be intimidating. We often solicit inexperienced people for the job and then expect them to lead, as if it were an effortless and natural thing to do. Maybe it is, for some. For many others, it definitely is not.

Potentially good leaders often flounder in the uncertainty of their roles. Or they sink under the weight of traditional norms that "must" be perpetuated. We often don't give them permission to be innovative or authority to delegate. We expect them to be "doers" to the point of martyrdom, and then we wonder why they seek early retirement.

The presiding officers of our church committees must know how to facilitate the group in a responsible way. They needn't be experts in parliamentary procedure, but they should understand the basic principles of committee management.

Sheila Albert of Sheila Albert & Associates in Santa Rosa, California, developed the following guidelines for effective committee chairs:

1. **Understand the committee's charge.** If it is not clear or convincing, ask. It may, in fact, need revising.

2. Meet only as often as necessary to accomplish the job, when there's **needed work that a group can do better than an individual.** Don't meet because it's Tuesday.

3. **Plan the agenda** enough in advance to allow it to be mailed to members 5-7 days in advance of meeting. Encourage members to be prepared; their time is better spent.

4. Allow sufficient agenda time to discuss important issues. Outline alternatives and implications. **Members want to participate, not "rubber stamp" decisions.**

5. If you have to miss a meeting, take the initiative to **select and orient a replacement.** Poorly led meetings discourage members and seldom accomplish much.

6. **Start all meetings on time.** Lead meeting in accord
   with agenda, controlling discussion so that all
   items have sufficient time. Postpone unfinished
   items if necessary. Clarify what actions are to be
   taken by whom before next meeting. **End on
   time.**

7. **You are a process manager, facilitator, listener.**
   Encourage participation of all members, drawing
   out quiet ones and tactfully limiting participation
   of those who tend to dominate. Hold your opinion until others have expressed theirs. Learn and
   practice these skills; they're difficult but possible.

8. **Orient new members** personally to committee purpose, issues and functioning. Help new people
   feel valued from the start and they will learn
   faster, be better integrated and move sooner into
   leadership.

9. **Use staff** well for their knowledge and expertise, but
   don't let them dominate. Your members will lose
   interest and you won't get what they could give.

10. Foster an **atmosphere of fun.** Work is more effec-
    tive when produced by people happily collaborat-
    ing. **Keep the energy high and positive.**

Should We Take Minutes?

We seldom think of recorded minutes as a
communication tool. That's because we mechanically
write them, absentmindedly approve them and then
permanently file them away. Taking minutes can
become such a cumbersome task that volunteers rank it

among their least favorite activities--right up there with meetings that last till midnight.

Minutes become a problem when:

a) we "lasso" someone into taking them at the last second (remember the Buffalo Bill theory), and/or

b) we require the recorder (whom we label "secretary") to produce a voluminous manuscript describing the meeting in meticulous detail, and/or

c) we require the reading aloud of said long-winded manuscript, and/or

d) we relegate the finished work to dusty archives after cursory approval

The first step in making good use of recorded minutes is to find a volunteer who doesn't mind taking them. Yes, there are people who actually enjoy the job. Creative writers often make wonderful reporters. If you want your committee's minutes to be entertaining as well as informative, find willing volunteers and give them a bit of poetic license. The pertinent facts and figures will be included and presented with interest, sometimes even humor.

Minutes need not be lengthy. A page--two at most--will accommodate the essentials of most meetings. A brief description of decisions made and actions taken is all that's really needed. Instead of detailed accounts of discussions, quick summaries of major points can be helpful.

Once we've gone to the trouble to record minutes, let's use them. Send a copy to anyone who missed the meeting, along with a personal note. Send copies as reminders of upcoming meetings, along with an agenda to help members prepare. You may want to give a copy of the minutes to the pastor and church staff members to keep them informed of your committee's activities. And don't forget to file a copy.

If the expense of copying and mailing minutes seems like an unnecessary one, consider the experience of one church that eliminated the practice to save money.

Church members were advised to check the newspaper and keep their calendars updated regarding meeting dates and times. Attendance at meetings fell off and continued a steady decline throughout the year. Finally the practice of making contact through the mail was reinstated.

Church leaders discovered that, rather than an extravagance, the messages communicated a sense of importance to the volunteer about his or her participation. It was a caring connection that provided the momentum some members needed in order to choose to attend.

Some churches print monthly calendars of volunteer activities. Others send volunteer newsletters. Use whatever method is most helpful to volunteers in your church. They will appreciate the consideration. You will like the results.

What Are Some Ways to Plan for Participation?

The last arrow I will aim at the way we conduct our church meetings is directed toward the sometimes haphazard way we plan goals and objectives and execute them. It's as though we are sure someone else will pick up the ball and run with it, assuming all the while that they know where the goal posts are.

Our group discussions become alarmingly predictable:

"Did you check with the pastor about the Bible presentation on Christian Education Sunday?"

"No. I thought you were going to do that."

"Well, let's be sure we get that done pretty soon."

"Good idea."

The same conversation will probably take place again at the next meeting. We're hesitant to delegate, hold volunteers accountable or make difficult decisions, because it seems incongruent with the image we have of ourselves as gentle Christian people. If our volunteer ministries are going to make a difference, we're going to have to adopt a more grownup attitude.

We must expect (and accept) disagreements. We can maintain high standards and expectations. We want to make use of volunteer expertise and should be willing to allow our committees the power to act. We can stop trying to please everybody. That's an impossible feat that isn't compatible with strong leadership, anyway.

Most of us don't generally associate risk-taking with church involvement. But all function requires risk. We can be so careful not to step on anyone's toes that we never get up out of the chair! You know how to be decisive and direct while remaining sensitive to others. That's the kind of leadership we need to model.

How Can We Plan & Conduct Successful Meetings?

The following guidelines will help keep volunteers involved and meetings productive:

Keep Information Flowing

Send a copy of the minutes to all committee members. Use colored paper and clip art to add interest. Outline any special assignments or important points with a highlighter pen.

Contact absentees to let them know they were missed. Ask for their assistance on a committee project.

Prepare an agenda and mail it to committee members a week before your scheduled meeting. Signify which items are for action and which for discussion.

Publish the committee meeting time, date and place in the church newspaper. List the committee members' names.

Allow Social Interaction

Designate the fifteen minutes **prior** to starting your meeting as a fellowship time. Have coffee, tea, lemonade, water, etc.
Foster a warm, congenial atmosphere. Smile. Use name tags, if necessary.

Have extra pencils.

Arrange **before** the meeting for a reporter to take notes.

Use a Printed Agenda

Start and stop on time as scheduled.

Keep opening remarks brief and informal.

Outline your expectations for the meeting.

Review agenda items. Accept additions only if time permits.

Set an approximate amount of time for each item. Be flexible, but move the meeting in a purposeful direction.

Use a chalkboard, charts or handouts as needed for greater understanding of complex issues.

See that everyone has an opportunity to speak. Don't let anyone dominate.

Work through disagreements.

Make decisions, design work plans, delegate responsibility and set a time frame.

Be affirming of individual viewpoints.

Close the meeting on a positive note.

Affirm Committee Members

Recognize contributions and accomplishments of members.

Encourage ideas and suggestions.

See that each volunteer has a role.

Tie in additional tasks to the mission statement.

Send thank-you notes for exceptional service.

Provide a nursery for all meetings and committee activities.

Thank all members for their participation and input.

Effective meetings are a vital factor in attracting and keeping volunteers. They show that we take our work--and our volunteers--seriously. We can plan for meetings that fill needs as well as accomplish goals. When we begin gathering for a specific purpose, we see the results in committed and enthusiastic volunteers.

It *is* possible to be both caring and efficient. Meetings that include both agendas and brownies are not necessarily working at cross purposes. And while it's true that churches aren't corporations, there is a definite need for some businesslike approaches if we are to achieve our objectives. The best intentions are never realized until they are translated into action.

Meetings that matter are the only ones worth having.

Chapter Nine

Creative Conflict: The Way to Lasting Agreements

The measure of success is not whether you have a tough problem to deal with, but whether it's the same problem you had last year.

John Foster Dulles

Therefore, putting away falsehood, let every one speak the truth with his neighbor, for we are members one of another.

Ephesians 4:25 (RSV)

The game of baseball intrigues me. Players, managers and umpires gather on a grassy diamond for the purpose of playing a game. The stands are full of happy spectators who paid money to participate. The atmosphere is charged with expectancy. A little healthy grime, loud music and an endless supply of hot dogs keep the fans happy. All is well. Then, in an instant, a fight breaks out on the field.

Players yell insults, hurl their caps to the ground, wave their arms, and sometimes throw punches. Like party crashers, other players join the fracas. The melee invades the stands, and ticket-holders chunk crumpled paper cups and empty popcorn boxes in a show of support or aggravation (I'm never sure which). Whether the issue is resolved or not seems immaterial. The conflict is aired and viewpoints are exchanged, albeit in a primitive manner.

As someone involved in both church administration and volunteering, I am repelled by this type of direct confrontation, while, at the same time, I'm strangely envious. In the church, we pride ourselves on sensitive diplomacy, but in reality, there are times when most of us long to scream and yell and throw our hats.

We don't, of course, and therein lies part of our problem.

Don't misunderstand. I'm not advocating fistfights or namecalling during committee meetings. But I do suggest an acceptance of confrontation in the church, where disagreements, misunderstandings and dissension *do* occur.

Naturally, we are afraid of hurt feelings and angry reprisals. But we cannot let that fear hold our volunteers and our programs hostage. The fact is that the more we refuse to recognize and deal with conflict, the more hurt and angry feelings there are.

Even people with excellent communication skills may hesitate to use them when problems arise in the church. Perhaps the arena seems inappropriate, or maybe the issues are emotionally charged. It could be that our understanding of our faith excludes acknowledging that conflict, both major and minor, is an inevitable part of people working together--even in the church.

So, by denying our feelings and guarding our interactions, we limit both vision and service. Our movements become predictable, and we adhere to only "safe" practices that don't offend anyone. Or we push our struggles underground, which makes them deadly.

Although conflict has negative connotations for many of us, there are positive aspects, as well. Through conflict come opportunity, growth, change, resolution, creativity, reconciliation and even bonding. Those things are as much a part of our Christian heritage as compassion, service, gentleness and love.

Is Conflict Inevitable?

By its very nature, the church is a diverse entity. The people who make it up are individuals. Our ideas and approaches vary. Inevitably, our priorities clash.

As individuals, we bring contrasting viewpoints, divergent philosophies and dissimilar work habits to all church programs. That fact, coupled with our interdependency of structure and purpose, creates conflict.

Disagreements can develop between individuals or between groups of individuals. Imagine the following scenario.

The New Membership Committee of a growing church recognizes the need to upgrade the nursery facilities. They are concerned about such matters as the limited number of cribs available and the need for training for the nursery staff.

The New Membership Committee instigates a process that will lead to change. They start with the Education Committee.

In a spirit of cooperation, the Education Committee studies the problems and develops two options for improving the nursery. They present both options to the Building and Grounds Committee, which in turn asks the Finance Committee to evaluate them. The Finance Committee rejects both options as too expensive.

At this point, the New Membership Committee members think the Finance Committee members are misers. The money-folks think the membership folks have no sense of practicality. Members of the other two committees wonder how they got caught in the middle of the squabble and hope nobody remembers they had any part in it.

All these groups have a vested interest in solving the problem.

Issues like this are not simply a matter of individual or interpersonal conflicts; they go to the very root of a congregation's sense of mission and vision for ministry! The process of resolving them may be fraught with conflict.

Conflict. Like the foreigner who walked up to two men playing Frisbee is a New York park and asked, "Who's winning?", we tend to see a problem as a win/lose proposition. But conflict is neither good nor bad; like a game of Frisbee, it simply *is*.

So what are the possibilities for our clashing committees? If the church is to grow, it must somehow upgrade nursery facilities.

To reach a resolution satisfactory to all, the committee members must work through the alternatives available to them together. They must explore in many different directions.

Perhaps they can work together to organize a special fund raising campaign.

Maybe they can break the project into stages and fund one part at a time.

In talking it over, they may discover that they need a larger nursery more than they need a giant library, and simply switch the two rooms.

Or they may decide to rent the empty office space across the street, rather than build another room.

But they'll never discover that any of these alternatives exist if they can't admit to themselves that conflict exists. Once they can do that, they can agree to disagree long enough to work out a mutually satisfactory resolution. And they'll find their ministry enhanced by the process.

Such struggles may encompass a large number of

church volunteers and stir up quite a controversy. Other conflicts are smaller, and they may be less intense. Or they may not be. Consider the situations described below:

> PROBLEM: Mark thinks the food bank should stay open during the lunch hour, but Marsha feels insecure, because no other church personnel will be in the building at that time.

> POSSIBLE SOLUTIONS: 1) Recruit more volunteers for the noon hour so that Martha won't have to be alone. 2) Have church staff members stagger their lunch hours. 3) Ask a local security business to donate the services of an employee for one hour.

> PROBLEM: Diane likes the idea of a church Halloween carnival, but Cliff would rather the church not recognize the holiday.

> POSSIBLE SOLUTIONS: 1) Call it an All Hallow's Eve Festival. 2) Celebrate All Saints' Day instead. 3) Have participants come dressed as Biblical characters and saints.

> PROBLEM: Sylvia says the children's choir members look best with white stoles, but Jessie thinks red is more striking.

> POSSIBLE SOLUTIONS: 1) Rotate the colors each month. 2) Let the boys wear one color and the girls another. 3) Make new blue ones.

Do these problems and their solutions seem ridiculously simple? Well, they all took place. And if the situations described here strike you as trivial, it's for a very good reason. *They were dealt with before they escalated into major conflicts with hidden agendas.* When our communication is not open and honest, we tend to start collecting "ammunition" to support our position against our adversaries. These problems were not allowed to grow to that point.

Michael Murray, a volunteer consultant and trainer in Arlington, Texas, has this to say about human nature: "Whatever I believe to be true, I work incredibly hard to keep true, because I would rather be right and miserable than wrong and happy."

When volunteers experience a high level of discontent, their effectiveness is impeded and the church climate is undermined. As church leaders, we can help by acknowledging conflicts and modeling a direct approach for dealing with them.

How Can We Engage in Positive Conflict?

Elaine Yarbrough, Ph.D., of Yarbrough and Associates in Boulder, Colorado, serves as a consultant in communication and conflict management. In her seminars, she outlines several fundamental steps toward reaching good agreements.

1. Negotiations should produce wise agreements that consider the legitimate interests of all parties.

2. Positive conflict is efficient. It addresses the real issues and gets the job done faster.

3. Solutions should be durable, so that the same conflicts are not repeated over and over again. They are durable when the real, rather than the surface issues are discussed.

4. Agreements should take the good of the church into consideration.

5. Positive conflict should improve, or not damage, relationships. This, of course, does not mean that negative feelings, such as anger or sadness should be avoided. Rather, they should be owned and stated directly.

6. Close negotiations by getting good agreements that are specific and measurable. Include time tables.

In church, we often display such a desperate need for harmony that we shortchange the process of arriving at satisfactory agreements. We want to "be nice" and therefore end up saying and doing nothing. Or, in search of a consensus, we dilute our positions to the point that we lose sight of goals and possibilities. The resulting frustration can be polarizing.

To interrupt this nonproductive cycle, Mike Murray uses an exercise called "How to Go from a Gripe to a Goal in Five Minutes." He suggests writing answers to the following "fill-in-the-blank" statements in twenty-five words or less:

1. My gripe is that _____ .

   Or My frustration is that _____ .

   Or My difficulty is that _____ .

2. My real concern is that _____ .

3. What I'm really wishing for is _____ .

4. Therefore, my goal is to _____ .

To complete these four sentences, one must engage the entire personality (the child, parent and adult within each of us) in the problem-solving process. The exercise channels our energy in a positive direction, allowing us to keep working at defining the problem until we turn it into a goal.

Here are some guidelines to help make meetings productive:

Look for areas of agreement and name them. Write the common goal on a chalkboard. Try describing the other person's position without forming judgments or evaluations. This isn't easy. A friend of mine advises taking a "bird's-eye view" of conflict situations. That kind of distancing allows us to make observations without becoming embroiled in the dispute.

Share power. Negotiate fairly. A volunteer's perspective is as legitimate as a staff member's. Every person involved must have the opportunity to influence the decision.

See negotiators as human beings. Even the most stubborn people relax when scratching the family dog. The older gentleman who opposes the mentor program for young welfare mothers is probably a wonderful grandfather. We all look delightfully silly when blowing out the candles on our birthday cakes. Images like these help keep things in perspective.

Be in charge of yourself. Own your own thoughts and feelings, rather than naming "allies" to support your position.

Avoid past history. There is seldom good reason to bring up old disagreements when discussing current issues. Stick to what is relevant. See problems as they currently exist and decide where to go from there.

Think in terms of agreement, rather than winning. Progress comes from resolving an issue, not defeating an opponent. Use the mission statement to direct the discussion.

Use friendly persuasion. We can waste a lot of energy working to persuade others to see things our way. People in the church don't always have to understand each other to maintain respect and tolerance.

Not long ago, I waited in line behind an interesting man at the neighborhood cleaners. He was explaining to the clerk that he wanted his pants cleaned and repaired. He pointed out two ripped pockets, a frazzled hem and a tiny hole in a side seam. As the clerk finished tallying up the fees, he added, "I guess you'd better put in a new zipper, too."

Never in a million years would I have considered making such extensive--and expensive--repairs to an obviously ancient pair of pants. But what did I know? Maybe he always wore these particular pants on Saturdays; maybe his wife gave them to him; or maybe he once won a race while wearing them. I don't know!

It made no difference whether I *understood* the man's viewpoint or not. I did not have to try to persuade him that he could buy a new pair of pants on sale for what he was paying to have the old ones repaired. *I* didn't have to wear the pants or pay the repair bill. Although I didn't agree with his decision, I could accept it. And smile.

That sort of thing is going to happen in our volunteer programs, too. Every difference of opinion doesn't necessarily require confrontation. Many times, we can smile and let others do things their own way, whether we agree or not.

Some occasions that look like potential disasters turn out to be simple misunderstandings. A lecturer once told of beginning her speech before a large audience, when she noticed two people on the third row whispering to each other. She tried to ignore their behavior, but her irritation grew as it continued. Mentally, she made angry assumptions about their rudeness. After the speech, she was surprised when one of them approached her and said, "I hope you didn't mind my translating your speech for my friend. He doesn't speak a word of English."

The clearer we are as leaders and volunteers and as a church body, the better we function. And when areas of disagreement arise, we can tackle the toughest problems and still be a church.

Our goal is not necessarily to agree, understand or even empathize with each other's viewpoints. Our goal is to work together to carry out our mission. Our differences and our similarities can both further our ministries.

Disagreements are a part of life. They are also a part of volunteer programs and projects. Working through conflict is seldom easy, but when we learn to face problems with a sense of equanimity and cooperation, we build strong relationships that withstand controversy and produce satisfying results.

Chapter Ten

Clergy and Staff Support: How to Empower Disciples

A good boss makes people realize they have more ability than they think they have, so that they consistently do better than they thought they could.

Charles Wilson

But I am among you as one who serves.

Luke 22:27 (NIV)

Cows would have a better perspective if they could see the world from both sides of the fence. I know, because I've grazed in the pastures as a volunteer and roamed the fields as a church staff member. From either angle, I see tremendous changes occurring.

If present trends continue, the church of tomorrow will have a smaller staff. It will also have more direct involvement from volunteer leadership. That means that we must begin preparing now for the gradual shifting of power and influence that has traditionally remained in the clergy's domain. Volunteers will have to accept and make better use of the responsibilities given them. And church professionals will have to give up some control.

Don't misunderstand me. Most pastors have plenty to do without engaging in power struggles over volunteer programs! But the "doer" instinct has been cultivated in our clergy. I suspect it begins in divinity school and is enhanced by congregations who treasure the close contact with their ministers. Other church professionals share that instinct. I know I did. Until I became really, really tired.

Only then did I realize how many of my responsibilities could be shared with volunteers. It took a gargantuan effort to let go of some of the jobs I not only performed, but created. Giving up control was hard, but in the long run, it was better for the church and better for me.

The issue of control is not often a blatant tug-of-war. It's sometimes so subtle that we fail to recognize it. For instance, a member of the church staff may feel some resentment at being saddled with the job of poring over color samples for the new paint in the choir room. But often, subtle leadership patterns may have made it impossible for anyone else to make the decision.

Let's look at a further example. Suppose the worship committee wants to help the congregation participate more fully in the worship service. They decide to include the pew Bible page number alongside the Scripture reference in the worship bulletin.

Since the pastor is present at this committee meeting and says nothing to the contrary, the committee assumes that its decision will be implemented. It isn't.

The pastor does not want to offend committee members, but she has a fundamental philosophical objection to what she sees as "spoon-feeding" churchgoers. She hopes that if the page number is not listed, the congregation will be motivated to learn how better to use the Bible.

The conflict here has nothing to do with which position is "right." The issue is one of power. The fact that forthright communication never occurred further complicates the problem.

When church staff members regularly override decisions made by volunteers, they send a message to the congregation: "You may as well refer all matters to the church staff for approval or decisions to start with, because they are going to have the final say, anyway."

Often, the larger the church staff, the greater the conflict. The mindset in some churches is that members are paying for the leadership and service of experts who are expected to create, develop, implement and sustain all things significant. When things go haywire, members can blame the professionals. But there's no staff in the world that can guide a thriving, growing church without the energetic leadership that only the laity can provide.

Our theology tells us that *every church member is a minister*. There are some roles that only the clergy can perform. But there are many others that can challenge the full range of the congregation's expertise. That means that as a staff member or volunteer leader, I will sometimes allow someone else to perform a job or service that:

a) I am perfectly capable of doing,
b) I'm quite good at, and/or
c) I enjoy doing.

In their book, *Volunteer Youth Workers*, authors Stone and Miller write, "If a team is to function, we must let them get into the game."

How Can We Function as a Team?

Let's start with an example from the Education Department. As the director, I can...
recruit Sunday School teachers...
keep the supply room stocked...

provide training...
plan recognition events...
prepare mission projects...
schedule fellowship events...
write notes to visitors...
send birthday cards...
design and publish a monthly newsletter...
arrange field trips...
choreograph the Christmas pageant...
make cookies for the choir...
change the bulletin boards each quarter...
keep the scrapbook updated...
be in charge of acolytes...
teach Confirmation classes...
send publicity notices to the newspapers...
create new and exciting programs...

...and die young.

A healthier alternative would be to develop a "Resource Bank" of talented people who would donate their services for special occasions or on a short-term basis. I might coordinate the following positions for the Education Department's volunteer team:

photographer	secretary
historian	chair, Choir Boosters
culinary artist	newsletter editor/ publisher
field trip guide	party coordinator
pageant director	bulletin board designer
Confirmation leader	stock clerk
acolyte director	publicity chair
mission leader	special event coordinator

Etc. If my efforts are then supported by an active volunteer ministries program, the Education Department can do more, be more and have more fun. If all ideas and activities must be the work of one individual--volunteer or staff--then the program thrives only as long as the person in charge does. And at the hectic pace in many churches, that's not long.

As the director of the program outlined above, my willingness to let go of some control would be a significant factor. The tricky part is that I know that some volunteers will do their jobs better than I could have done them. Some will do them every bit as well. A few may not meet my expectations or get the job done at all. (This last is less likely to happen if the volunteer program has done its job of discovering gifts, interviewing and placing volunteers in jobs that are right for them.)

What often happens when the ball does get dropped, however, is that professional church members feel compelled to pick it up. Floundering projects make everyone nervous. But if I continually rescue inefficient volunteers, or if I step in every time a program falters, I bring control back into the professional court.

"If a team is to function, we must let them get into the game." Nobody wants to be a token player. If our volunteer recruitment efforts focus on finding the best person to do a job that he or she wants to do, then we will have few qualms about entrusting that person with leadership. We can step back and let the volunteer make decisions, knowing that the right to decide is a basic part of the job.

How Can Authority Be Used Wisely?

You can use your influence to encourage, affirm and claim the work of the volunteer in the church and the community. Support those who serve both publicly and privately. Elevate volunteer ministries to a place of importance in your church.

Many church leaders advocate a regular and systematic recognition of volunteers during times of worship and fellowship. Others make it a point to stay informed about who is serving where, so that they can stop by the workplace to say hello or can send a note of encouragement.

We spoke earlier in this book about the value of spotting potential. Church leaders with a capacity to see the best in people motivate volunteers to take risks and grow. They have faith in the abilities of others and show it by allowing volunteers to lead the church ministries.

Allow risk taking. Some of the most successful programs start out as radical concepts. One town took a chance. They took troubled teens, with histories of legal violations, and placed them with other young people living in a home for the physically and mentally disabled. And it worked.

The project made the teens feel needed and loved--some for the first time in their lives. The handicapped youths responded better to these new caregivers than they did to teachers who were trained to work with them. Everybody benefited.

But first, someone had to say, "Let's *do* it."

Trust that by enabling others to succeed, you enhance your own leadership. The "boss" who celebrates the accomplishments of other staff members or volunteers brings a joyful enthusiasm to ministry. If we are to move forward, the clergy and church leaders must cheer volunteers on--every step of the way.

Why Is Information Powerful?

The availability of information directly affects leadership. Appropriate channels of communication are vital for the exchange of information from staff to volunteers and vice versa.

If a brochure arrives announcing a seminar on marketing volunteer programs, will the staff Volunteer Coordinator notify committee chairs and project leaders? Does the church secretary make his or her clip art files available to volunteers? Is the resource library unlocked on Sunday mornings and during meetings?

Information often equals power. Relinquishing control of it sometimes comes down to the question of whether I, as a leader, am willing to allow another to know as much about a subject as I do. More often, it's a question of simply remembering to disperse information to those who might benefit. Sharing information is one important way to empower disciples.

The best leaders--clergy or lay--delight in the success of others. No one corners the market on good ideas when leaders and volunteers support and encourage each other. The concept of the servant/leader that Jesus modeled so well helps us keep our roles in perspective and our priorities in line.

What Are Some Ways to Focus on Volunteers?

Have you noticed that when a pastor or staff person enters a committee meeting or planning session, the focus in the room shifts slightly toward that person? It may be almost imperceptible. Heads may incline slightly in a new direction. Chairs may be scooted back to ensure the newcomer a clear line of sight. Questions may be directed toward that person, rather than addressed to the chairperson or group leader.

Sometimes, when a church professional enters a meeting in progress, the atmosphere itself changes. There may be less freedom of expression, less spontaneity. There may be subtle responses within the group to the staff person's mood.

It's not that the professionals are intentionally overbearing--not at all. Title and position alone are often enough to affect group dynamics.

The same might hold true to a lesser degree for chairpersons sitting in on subcommittee meetings--the group leader ceases to be in charge, as if by some unspoken code.

If, as leaders, our attendance at certain meetings is mandatory, we need to find ways to take a back seat throughout proceedings chaired by someone else.

Many meetings do not require clergy or staff presence at all. There are other, more efficient ways to keep up with what's going on in all areas of the church.

It's always a judgment call as to whether clergy or staff presence is needed in any particular meeting. But many options exist between close supervision and a total "hands-off" approach. Pastors and other staff members will need to decide how much control to exercise in any given situation. It is to be hoped that the work of the church can rest in the hands of carefully chosen leaders. But there will be times when closer supervision is required. Most church professionals work hard to maintain a delicate balance.

As lay people, it's important for us to recognize that the "success" of the church directly affects a pastor's career. The clergy have a tremendous investment in our collective ministries, and in us as individuals, as well. We help them do their jobs by doing ours.

Who Are the Likable Leaders?

What kinds of traits inspire volunteers? Probably the same ones that you yourself appreciate in leaders who have helped you. A group of one hundred volunteers created the lists below:

What We Like	What We Dislike
accessibility	intimidation
honesty	unfairness
organization	cynical attitude
sense of humor	moodiness

What We Like	What We Dislike
accepts respon- sibility for own mistakes	won't share infor- mation
flexibility	demeaning remarks
a good listener	critical
shows concern and interest	patronizing
team player	fosters discontent
delegator	says yes without meaning it

Volunteers in the church, probably more than anywhere else, care what supervisory personnel think about them and the work they do. STAFF OPINIONS MATTER! Congregations develop deep attachments to their pastors. They seek their approval, but, more importantly, they desire their respect. The confidence that leaders place in volunteers' ability to do the jobs entrusted to them communicates high regard.

Leaders can show their interest in volunteers by inviting them to staff meetings to explain a project, give a progress report or provide input in a question under discussion. Leaders can ask for help in evaluating programs and planning for the future. Leaders can express their personal appreciation for a volunteer's service. And leaders can celebrate every area of volunteer ministries in the church and the community.

Church professionals have the ability to influence attitudes and impact climates. They help by encouraging innovation. They help by lending enthusiasm to creative ideas and new directions. They help by assisting others to anticipate change with optimism. Staff attitudes can pave the way for acceptance and success of volunteer programs. Those programs must have staff support to succeed.

How Can We Turn Maintenance into Mission?

On a scale of one to ten, where would you place the importance of your current volunteer program in the minds of the congregation? Do they see it as a cumbersome but necessary part of keeping the church going?

If so, you might want to ask yourself some further questions. How does the present leadership facilitate volunteer action? How widespread are opportunities for serving beyond the local church? How much fun is the congregation having?

Church administrators hold the key that opens the door to volunteer involvement. Leaders must be managers, enablers, cheerleaders and innovators. They must know when their voices need to be heard and when to remain silent. Above all, leaders must be seen as those who serve.

Granting others the option of service is allowing them to make a difference. Volunteers bring the Gospel to life. Even if they make mistakes. Even if every effort is not a colossal success. Even if you or I would have done things differently.

Your volunteer ministries program makes disciples out of ordinary human beings. The church has the structure, the expertise, the people and the mission to create a better world. The time has come to gather our resources and heed God's call.

Shall we sound the trumpets?

Suggested Readings

Children as Volunteers, by Susan J. Ellis, Editor, Katherine N. Noyes, Trina Tracy and Lawrence Wallace. Energize, 1983.

The Church that Cares, by Kenneth R. Miller and Mary Elizabeth Wilson. Judson Press, 1985.

Dealing with Difficult Volunteers, by Marilyn MacKenzie. Heritage Arts Publishing, 1988.

How to Make the World a Better Place, by Jeffrey Hollender. William Morrow, 1990.

How to Mobilize Church Volunteers, by Marlene Wilson. Augsburg Publishing House, 1983.

101 Tips for Volunteer Recruitment, by Steve McCurley and Sue Vineyard. Heritage Arts Publishing, 1988.

Volunteer Youth Workers, by David Stone and Rose Mary Miller. Group Books, 1985.

Volunteer Management Resources

Association for Creative Change
NTRI, PO Box 1022
405-210 College Ave.
Clemson, SC 29633

The Center for Creative Community
PO Box 2427
Santa Fe, NM 87504-2427

Heritage Arts VM Systems
1807 Prairie Ave.
Downers Grove, IL 60515

Michael F. Murray
Creative Interchange
Consultants International, Inc.
1018 Arlena Drive
Arlington, TX 76012

Volunteer Impact: New Ideas for Growing Churches
A bimonthly newsletter
421 Sam Rayburn Fwy. N.
Sherman, TX 75090

Volunteer Management Associates
Marlene Wilson, President
320 S. Cedar Brook Rd.
Boulder, CO 80304

Acknowledgements . . .

One of the things I like best about the volunteer management field is the willingness of the experts to share freely what they know. This book is a combination of their wisdom and my experience.

A special thanks to Marlene Wilson, a mentor to many. Without her contagious enthusiasm and desire to help others succeed, this book would not have been possible.

Kudos to Mike Murray, who challenged me to take some risks and chart a new direction.

Warmest regards to all the volunteer managers and church leaders around the country who told me their stories and impressed me with their knowledge and professionalism.

Finally, I extend my deepest appreciation to Jessie Stephens, my editor and friend. Her faith in me, and her admonitions to shorten my sentences, made this book a readable reality.

Index

Did you borrow this book? Want a copy of your own?

Yes! I want to invest in the future of my volunteer ministries. Please send me my own personal copy of *Volunteer Ministries: New Strategies for Today's Church.* I'm enclosing $15.95, which includes postage and handling. Publisher will pay sales tax, where applicable.

Send my book to me at:

Name:_____

Church (if purchasing with church funds):_____

Street:_____

City/St/Zip:_____

Send check payable to: Newton-Cline Press
                         421 N. Sam Rayburn
                         Sherman, TX 75090

Quantity Orders Invited
For bulk discount prices call (214) 892-1818

Volunteer Impact: New Ideas for Growing Churches

A national bimonthly newsletter edited by Margie Morris...a one of-a-kind-resource for church volunteer directors and coordinators. News, tips, guidelines, answers to your questions and more...

Yes! I want to invest in the future of my volunteer ministries. Please start my subscription to *Volunteer Impact* today. I'm enclosing $20 which includes postage and handling.

Send my subscription to me at:

Name:_____

Church (if purchasing with church funds):_____

Street:_____

City/St/Zip:_____

Send check payable to:　Newton-Cline Press
　　　　　　　　　　　　421 N. Sam Rayburn
　　　　　　　　　　　　Sherman, TX 75090